THEN A MIRACLE

LOVE STORIES

ROD MAGNER

FOREWORD

If you have found in your life experiences that seem for all the world to be as much a miracle as any other explanation, then you may smile at some of what I have here.

I filled many yellow pads over the years, just for myself to re-read at my leisure. Some of those were streams of consciousness and a couple of those are here. I have also always enjoyed someone's unique phraseology for something I had not encountered before and if any of those quotes are here, I apologize if they are not properly attributed.

My father taught me when I was about 10 what a googol was, a 1 with one hundred zeroes after it. A number with more than the number of elementary particles in the Universe. Everywhere I turn I see aspects of that mind-boggling number, and I think Miracles are equal in number.

Life itself is the Miracle which works for me. Where did the first spark of life originate, which confluence of quarks brought forth the very first wiggle that became us? If the Universe is expanding, what is it expanding into? If we live a third of each day in a dream state, why only a third? Why is there something rather than nothing?

I think we are finding out. Maybe a global consciousness is wiggling its way into our so-called individual consciousness, one that was never separate, simply hidden by a thin veneer of imagination, or old stardust.

Table of Contents

TIRE SWING

1965

I'd swing with you Sweetheart,
on an old tire swing
I'd swing you high
as high as I could
Long as you cared to the ride the old thing
Come my turn, if you would
Spin me around and let her fly
I love to spin, I don't know why
We wore the earth under that swing,
Dragging our feet through time,
Me swinging you, you swinging me
Love singing from eternity
I'd swing you Sweetheart
As long as I could, in the shade of that tree
Just me swingin' you, you swingin' me.

WHITE BIRD

I asked later, how did this bird find its way into my life, and why did it come when it did? What was it trying to teach me? Those were the kinds of questions one asks when the memories of the first encounter flash before you as if it were today, not ten years beyond that life changing moment. It was so simple I did not see it clearly, for it was much less than what it would become. I see it plainly now, and the story can be told.

She was mostly white, her feathers a pure white radiance that filled the space around her as water fills a vessel and then overflows. The aura spilled into the air like the scent of a familiar perfume. As I reached down to pick her up I expected my hands to begin glowing. As I moved them silently towards her resting place in the tall green grass, her head shifted so that one deep blue eye could watch me. I expected to find her trembling, or to flutter up in my face and screech in terror. None of that happened.

I lifted her gently, both hands wrapped firmly around her back and wings. She offered no resistance, in fact, she seemed to soften and mold her body to my grasp, as if no one in the world had held her and she had been waiting for this moment to learn the touch of human form.

Her gaze never wavered. I held her at eye level in the afternoon sun, our eyes locked in a mystical embrace. She was injured, but I did not know where. Beneath the soft white feathers of her chest I felt a heart beating in tune with mine. It was nearly calm, and in some way, self-assured, passing its peace on to me.

I relaxed my grip upon her back, and cradled her in one hand, stroking her head while running my fingers down her back, then across her wings. She was the most remarkable bird I had ever seen. My quiet inspection of her flying feathers showed them all intact. Through all my efforts she offered no resistance.

I carried her a few yards to the silver maple guarding the corner of the summer pasture, tall with green grass. I sat in cool shade at the base of the tree and placed her in my lap.

I could find no visible sign of physical injury. None. During this whole encounter, her piercing gaze never left me. From the trust I was experiencing I sensed the hurt was inside her. From the sunlight that reflected off her in little splashes of rainbow, she conveyed to me she was quietly healing. I smiled at the thought as it danced across my consciousness. I was certain I was right, but no words existed to confirm it.

How long would it take her to heal I wondered? What if I became attached to her in the meantime? I laughed at myself suddenly. In the first instant I spotted her lying in the grass, I felt a warm kinship which did not form into words or come from them. It simply found expression through our eyes, wings and fingers, and beating hearts. I had become attached the moment we connected, and once again in my life, I was about to learn something. Birthed from every previous attachment had come new lessons.

We shared the isolated summer afternoon, touching and wondering and all without a spoken word. Patiently we waited, hard against the bark of the maple, pulling up a few blades of grass and watching cumulus build to the north.

In those few hours of that July day, wrinkles in my thinking were mystically organizing into clear patterns. Troubles that had made my life a mine field filled with frustrations dissolved into the air, distilled like dew on a spider's web. Together we had grown and healed each other. This fragile white bird whose species is unknown to me, rested in my lap and without a sound, told me truths about myself I was ready to accept.

As the sun began to color the early evening sky, I felt a change in her. She seemed to resonate with a new energy, a tentative restlessness. The moment was approaching, I knew, for our parting. Now, this warm, loving creature rested in my lap, yet in the next instant, there would be only a warm impression, and perhaps a feather.

I wanted to cry, echoing a deep sadness and a profound joy. My breath caught in my chest as she stretched slowly first one wing, then the other. For the first time her eyes moved from mine and scanned the crimson sunset to the west. Then her eyes returned once again to mine and she soothed the heartache and loss I felt coming.

Mysteriously the pain did not come. In its place, a pure white love that was ready to fly again, unfettered, free of every obstacle in its path. We had healed each other.

I raised her up with both hands and drew my face close to hers. "Thank you!" I said. She blinked an eye, seemed to bow her tiny head, then with little catches of her claws turned slowly in my palms.

In a flutter of iridescent white wings, she rose into the evening sky. Circling once in a wide arc, she paused, and with her wings straight, silhouetted against the fading light, began a glide directly towards me. Suddenly she uttered a cry of absolute joy, a sound so pure it lives as a singularly perfect hymn in my heart.

Did I ever see her again? Yes. Often? Yes, whenever I needed her, or she needed me.

And when was that? Whenever we needed to learn about Love, to be reminded how free it is, how pure it must remain, how wordless it can be.

SOMEWHERE IN TIME

Standing alone on the Paris street corner, the old man paused to gaze at the Parisian skyline which included the Eiffel Tower a few blocks away. It seemed to point in a direction which had been the cardinal heading of his long life. The rain swept passed him tonight in a gentle wind. It filled the gutters with tiny streams sailing dark oily leaves, the remnants of fall, harbingers of winter. Though his slouch hat tried, it could not prevent his glasses from becoming dotted with the crystal-clear raindrops.

His head turned away to check traffic before stepping off the curb. At 2AM, midweek in December, he saw only a single car three blocks away, its headlights distorted through his rimless glasses. It posed no threat to his simple crossing of the Rue de Drout. Just blocks from home now, a tiny walkup apartment with a stunning view of the Seine.

The morning sunlight streaming in the living room window was its salvation. It made the small space and his life, larger by some quantifiable measure. Though he did not drink coffee, nor did she, the play of light through his tall morning glass of orange juice was a sundial for the two of them. Its shadow circled the table playfully, as if time were unimportant, merely a simple asterisk to life.

The memory of their meeting slid across his mind, silken and frictionless, yet as clear this moment as ever. Undimmed...She slept tonight, somewhere in time, warming the spot they would share when he returned from his walk. Unable to sleep, he had slipped away to fill his lungs with the Paris night air and his mind with the jetties of time that had pierced the veil to bring them together so many years before.

He knew that she would hear the soft clank of the tumbler in the door lock. His carefully muffled footsteps, the creak of the wood soaked in time. Yet she would say nothing, her eyes closed, her heart content, awaiting the slow motion of his return. He brought with him the soul cleansing night air, the fragrance of living life to its fullest. She offered in return a timeless love born in a Universe beyond their imaginings.

As the old man lay his head on the pillow, she drew his arm across her chest. No words were spoken. Only the soft sigh of the Universe in them could be heard across time.

A SMALL AND DISTANT FLUTTER

He could only see through the fog in the direction of the sunrise. Mornings like this were made by the Gods with airbrush perfection. Shafts of sunlight scattered the painted blanket of sky with old memories and his thoughts of a new beginning. She would never understand his passion for freedom. His freedom was too often her jailer. Locked in some embering fire of love that began in his youth, the truth of something so elusive as love only began to cast its long shadow as he approached the furthest side of fifty.

It no longer mattered. There was a mission ahead, for the day, for the year, perhaps for the rest of his life. This was the first day and in some abstruse way, he felt linked to forces that had moved minds always. Propel yourself toward that which you care most about. The simple notion followed the lines on the road ahead, like arrows.

She, Linda, felt it was all BS. And it was *his*. It was not a word she used to finish many sentences. The stuff to her was literal and filled the apartment they had shared for 10 years. Conversations between them had evolved into shoveling contests. In the closets, the carport, the kitchen cabinets, wedged between the washer and dryer, they had piled the droppings of humorless living. She had not yet tired of it, the warped logic of which escaped her. He headed south today. She was headed north.

James flipped off the radio. Seattle traffic was of no concern. Nor would it ever be. He had never really been a commuter anywhere he had lived. It would have been an assault on his time and he sidestepped the problem. Today he was looking for a single antique. Following a lead discarded in conversation with a bookseller one week earlier. Hung in a barn. Engineless. Old fabric would peel from its ribs and longerons.

The skeleton of a bird draped across a barbed wire fence where sun and wind weathered the calcium to a porous white labyrinth. What parts would remain and had not already followed the second law of thermodynamics to oblivion? The intrigue for him was abnormal. Searching through fog and countryside in out of the way places made him laugh with the world. There was no better life, no freer soul than he when he turned off the ignition down a long gravel driveway and looked across the mist filled barnyard at the Mail Pouch barn.

The front door knock went unanswered. The screen door had one football sized hole and the door twisted as he let it clatter shut. It was, to his way of thinking, a miracle, this peeling green door. The sound of its hinges was summer in Minnesota. The rust on the hinges was the work of a natural artist whose palette was time. He wanted to work the door some more, but that appeared, even to him, an awkward thing if he should be asked to explain it to anyone who might suddenly appear. He drew a long breath and turned to scrutinize the barn.

It matched the description. He made up his mind quickly. Peek inside, quietly. If he had to, he would say he had knocked. This farm was no longer a farm, simply its ghost image. An island of thought cutoff from the mainland. The forces of nature and the pressures of the marketplace wore out its heart. The massive main door was open enough for a handhold.

Friction of 100 years on the rollers at the door top. Open it just enough to squeeze inside, yet open enough to avoid unexplainable appearances. Inside, the late October morning light swept away patches of dark. Old hay. Alfalfa

—

centuries old. Dust and just then, a small and distant flutter. No song. No vision of it. Only an ancient invitation. Disturb the universe at rest, and you will hear it and feel it. A tiny quiver. A welcome and a warning.

The hay mow at the west end was nearly empty. On the east across the oil stained and broken concrete lay his quest. In the most distant corner, the shadow of a wing and the outline of a fuselage. A circumscribed dream littered with feathers and further principles of which James knew he was only vaguely aware. He crossed the interior slowly, letting his eyes adjust and his heart slow down. And there, again, the flutter of wings somewhere behind him.

It was indeed a TravelAir. He laughed out loud. It was the simple joy of "Aha." The freedom of life caught in a moment of great and unbridled discovery. It was what James craved most in life. Here, now, this utterly silent moment, his alone, face to face with the history of love hung from great curved rungs and listing to port like an old Victory ship. He stood a respectful distance away in prayer like contemplation.

"You know a TravelAir when you see one?" she said from behind him. James died a very quick death.

Leaning against the open barn door, silhouetted against October. She didn't wait for his answer, simply turned and leaned her weight against the door, shoving it full open to admit a blaze of sunlight. "I have ten minutes before I leave for town. Look it over carefully. She last flew 42 years ago. Landed just the other side of the barn and been in here ever since. She's yours if the price is right." She turned and headed for the house.

"Ooohh Kay...I'll do that!" Mystery and drama and quiet all shattered in an instant. The spell broken, but permission granted. He heard the screen door bang shut. And then caught the perfume. Woman. Farmwoman. He laughed out loud again. "Whose?" he thought.

James touched the wood and fabric that October. But he didn't touch her. He bought the antique, sold his financial freedom. But he was unwilling so quickly to sell his soul to this mist of a woman. She had a name. She filled the days to come with long words and muscle in the barn, and hot chocolate between hands with red nails.

He called her a farmwoman. "Janet Ross you are a farmwoman," he told her, "worthy of graffiti sprayed on construction walls." Sometimes he would hear, after she had left, the flutter of distant wings. In the middle of the barn now practically his home, he stood one cold February day and declared to himself that love, as he knew it so far, was all that mattered in the world. He bent to the task of resurrection, lofting freedom with wings and fabric to the reaches of his soul.

Janet Ross left one day. Smiled and bounced off down the long gravel driveway. James loved his freedom and there would be no hay in the barn of his soul to lie upon and think about life. About life together at least. Her blonde hair and red nails and farmwoman ways.

Colors and habits, he would paint into his airplane, so it would be gentle to him, feed him and his lonely soul, his free soul. And she would be free as well. One June day he would cut the hay and clear a path for takeoff and she would be somewhere else.

The TravelAir was a work of art. A splash of vibrant color across the June sky. Polished and poised and waiting. Red for Janet's nails. Yellow for her hair. From behind the reception desk at the Farmers Coop, Janet Ross could hear something small, something distant, a flutter in her heart. Looking out the window she knew what it was now. She crossed her legs and took out a nail file with a smile pursing her "passion red" lipstick painted lips.

FROM THE BEGINNING OF TIME

April 10, 1972

Lord his scream was piercing.

She held him nearly upside down, by his feet. The nurse stood in the far corner of the delivery room. He was red and cheesy, and his face was a big frown from one corner to the other.

"He's a healthy one," said the business as usual nurse. I looked over at him from beside the bed on which his mother lay exhausted but fully aware. This moment, this brief arrangement of characters, people holding new life aloft to be examined, to be loved, to be exalted, forever etched in memory.

Arms and legs unbending, flicking randomly. The nurse hands him to me wrapped in soft white blanket. He is mine. He is not mine. He is the world's; the world is his now. The journey has begun, with vision, with sound, with love and with noise wrapped in echoes of eternity. He weighs 8 pounds, 10 ounces. He weighs nothing. He has come to us from the beginning of time. I am his guide. He is my partner. We will grow again. Together. We share the same birthday. Only his now seems important.

Alison reaches out to treasure this child, this life she has known better than I. Together they cradle one another in a language of movement and soft sounds, a harmony of Love I feel stirring from deep inside me, a thing I observe from a distant galaxy from within me. Life constantly renewed, refreshed, uncorrupted. Whispering through the halls of evolution to this white washed hospital room. I am yours, you are mine, we are ever one. So, let us begin.

I leave the University Hospital at 2AM. In the car, alone, in the dark, I feel light. I am so proud. I have a son. I HAVE A SON. Dear sleeping town of Ann Arbor, WE... HAVE... A... SON! Only the street lights hear my exultation, the shout inside our old green Plymouth Barracuda. Four blocks from home, this clear sparkling night, this first night of new life, I run out of gas. Ease the car to the side of the road, latch the doors, laughing, crying, breathing deeply. I listen to my footsteps now. I hear more than my own. The crisp air courses through me in sweet profusion. Lucky to go home this way, an internal engine guiding me, stars for companions. Will it always be thus?

May 8, 1971

FRATERNITY

October 1964

At our annual fraternity alumni dinner, we sat as undergraduates and listened to the older, wiser brothers dispense wisdom. We could only learn at great expense, i.e. a Saturday night without a date. A sacrifice for the brotherhood.

I sat with one older brother who had been an Air Force F106 pilot and was now a banker. I told him I wanted to fly multiengine, try for the airlines later.

"That's OK, I guess, but let me tell you something…there's nothing better than flying fighters." His eyes grew misty in his head, his hands came up high and level and then said, "Can you do this with a P3 at 40,000 feet?" He rolled his palm up and flew inverted. Then he pulled it down in a smooth arc to the boardroom table. His huge grin hid some years of something that I knew I felt. What struck me, what I never forgot, was the idea of being able to roll upside down at 40,00 feet. Yes. that would be something, it really would.

Years later, on a weekend cross country with my A7, at 35,000, I rolled inverted as I passed an airliner coming in the opposite direction. I smiled, remembering my fraternity brother…

B52

Flying around my room in high school was bizarre collection of aircraft. Dangling from the ceiling directly over my head was a B-52 moving silently in the air that wafted through my bedroom. My flashlight at night crafted shadows that twisted slowly and flew on their own. Holding the models and hand flying them in carefully constructed patterns, I flew many hours before the day I sat in my first cockpit, alone.

Khrushchev was at the UN, banging his shoe on the table. It was called the cold war.

JETS DECISION

I have completed the Navy Preflight training, scorched through in good time and with good grades. Pete Cruiser and I spend lots of time on Pensacola Beach. Don Schafer and others are done too and the conversation centers on new "orders" due out on Friday. My real first choice is P3's. I want to fly big aircraft and go fly for an airline someday and live happily ever after.

"Come on, don't be an asshole, you don't want to fly T-28's at Whiting. Go jets man!" They say I won't believe how fantastic they are!

They're right, I don't want T-28's but P3's sound nice. All my friends are trying for jets. If I put jets as my first choice I've got it because my grades are excellent. I put my pen on the box marked jets. Everybody smiles.

Don Shafer spins in 3 months later, on his first night solo in a T2A jet at Meridian. Stupid. Shouldn't have happened! Damn sonofabitch. A wrestler from Ohio State, a crazy nice guy who absolutely loved to fly.

Thereafter I found myself in church rarely, just whenever somebody bought the farm.

So, a couple more times in the training command...

—

MY LIFE BY THE NUMBERS

4/10/1944 born
11 moved to Long Island summer 1955
14 first glider lesson
16 solo in Cub
17 private pilot license
1962 graduate high school
1966 graduate college
5/68 get wings in Navy
1/1/69 first combat mission
214 total carrier landings
60 night carrier landings
123 combat missions
5/8/71 married Alison
4/10/72 Scott born
10/8/75 Ryan born
10,000 landings in Magic
20,000+ passengers
7000 hours in Magic
19 CVA USS Hancock
2 Grandsons

SEASONS IN A DAY

September 10, 1982

Summer. Cold. Unusually cool. Dark thunderheads, anvil shaped spread east. Tops 60,000 feet. Glaciated. Hail inside. Probably ten miles across. Sweeping the ground with gale force. Driving curtain of rain. Solid, grey, loud. Stinging. Lightning everywhere, ricocheting off canyon walls. Splattering light and rolling thunder across a frenzy. Alone in this primeval holocaust. It can't last. it will pass. There we be a stillness, a wet quiet, soaking, curling green humid air. A drying period. A burst of sunlight, hot warming, bright. A wish then almost for the coolness before the storm.

Idle. Looking up. The wall retreats. You be here I thought. Be here with me. This living. Witness to force, to green wet black strength. The creation of earth. I was there, and a cowboy stood on his horse on the horizon, bemused by it.

Two inches below the crest of grass and dead leaves and insects, a black small creature scurried about. No apparent logic to his route. Moving in the frequency of life set at the far end of creations dial. Alone.

The tramp of boots. Squish. Dead insect. Cycle of living revolving once more. Tramp tramp, across an illusion of separateness. Huddle beneath a score of others concern. Dry, quick steps to get home. Television. Lost feeling, summer, every day a same one. Same damn one.

YOU ARE A LESSON IN TIME

Navy Flight Training

The car sailed quietly over the black two-lane backwoods road that ran north between Meridian and Starkville, Mississippi. Weekends were mine. To drive one hundred miles north and strap myself into a single seat sailplane.

I loved the flying. No instructors to critique me, no debrief, no mission plan. All that was necessary was thermal heat. To soar alone above the green carpet forests of Mississippi, alone with the great buzzards and hawks.

Early on Saturday morning; horse drawn buckboards headed into town, dusty brown feet of children swinging off the rear of the beds. I smiled at them, slowed, waited my chance to pass. Wanted to stay there, slow, dreaming with them as they bounced in unison, heads moving side to side; eyes questioning me, lips smiling.

I am a jet pilot you know...

We are traveling this world at such different speeds; here in my Pontiac, you on your gray old buckboard, me with twin speakers, you with ears to the natural world. I have slowed to join you, will you speed up ever, to be with me in my world? The buggy pulls off to one side when it can. I toot and pass and wave in my mirror. They have time to think.

They slip through life on the slow wheel of time and fortune, I spin through on a hot turbine, leaving residue and noise. But I do love you Mississippi. Your kudzu green and red orange earth rolling away hills dark starry nights. Tin shacks on stilts, dusty red barren yards, smoke curling from chimneys. You are a lesson in time, in poverty of "things" yet rich in natural pine forests.

I cannot speed past the farmer plowing wind and earth with a single blade behind a sweating horse the sun rising over his shoulder. You there, I am going to fly a sailplane today, for hours. I will soar above this earth you carve so carefully. I will etch lines of effort in the sky while you create the patterns of ribboned earth I use for palette.

We are both conspirators, both actors on this stage we have set up for rehearsal. I want to know the feel of the earth, the soil in my hand, my fingernails black with dirt. You want to fly, to join the column of sky that holds a promise of freedom. Perhaps we should talk, share these dreams of ours.

I could not know that this day I would nearly die in a thunderstorm. Smashed and battered by my own stupidity. Whipped and lashed by wind, my ship holds together, her wings taut. It is all I can do to land her in the teeth of the storm. Friends run and grab the wings. I have been foolish.

And that evening, I will recount with a date from the college in Starkville, the thrill of the day; build an image I must maintain for sanity, and for years to come. I drift home the way I came. Past poverty, past beauty, past the past.

When will life begin to make sense?

I am so full of life, trapped by its anomalies, but eager to learn her secrets. And there, there ahead is another buggy, life plodding along behind it. Would they pick up a hitchhiker... me?

I could park the Lemans forever, learn the guitar, walk the hot summer back roads, plant corn, watch the buzzards soar, weather the storms under a corrugated roof. Sweat, get thirsty, drink red pop, listen to the preacher, fish the Tombigbee. Old muddy river twisting through Life.

Tell me, please, just whisper it... why do I fly; what is it I love; where are you taking me?

RUNWAY 3-4

I roll out to line up on the runway for takeoff. In the warm sun I can smell the tread marks on the asphalt. There is not another plane in the sky. I am oh so ready for this. My day's assignment complete, the freedom of the sky mine to savor.

The world is quiet. So quiet. The airport is mine alone. All the lessons, my intuitions, complex theories, they vanish to my wingtips.

My tailwheel clanks on the hard surface as I finish the turn.

It is so quiet. As if the world has taken a mighty breath and held it. I hear only the distant shore and feel the rustle of air on my nose.

My heart, so full of love for my friends who have taught me what it means to be Free, is pumping with a singular purpose.

THE MYSTERY

No one can prepare you for her. The time and the place are not yours to decide. You may prepare the way, study what interests you, become passionate about a particular avocation. Run through life with your focus on destiny, self-scripted and plain for all to see.

When you least expect her, she will slip quietly into your consciousness, a feather on the wind. She will brush your cheek with angelic smiles and your eyes will ask in watercolor pastels, where have you been? Did we have to wait this long?

Yes and No... No and Yes. There is only NOW to capture the magic.

Finally! Real magic.

The chemistries of love dictate my day.

If I love what I am doing it is always obvious to an observer.
  If I love an object it is called desire.
   If I love the scent of the air it is called a memory.
    If I love a person in general, it is called compassion.

When I love a woman, I set in motion a universe of all possible constructions, chemical, physical, mystical and timeless.

Why evolution has set this complex task at my doorstep has only one answer.

The binding of the future to the past in a seamless, effortless NOW.

When I love her alone, eternity is a picnic with cosmic intentions. When I am in thrall of this curious magic, this dance for two, I am indeed,

In LOVE

The simple truth…it is…All my LOVE, every day.

FROZEN

I was frozen in disbelief at what the airspeed indicator read. A moment before I had been climbing in a right turn at 250 knots, complimenting my piloting skill inside a large chunk of nasty Chinese cumulus. This was my third combat flight and I was too nervous to be scared and too dumb to be smart enough to know why I was there. The airspeed indicator was winding past 450 knots. The standby gyro about the size of a quarter down in a forgotten corner of the instrument panel told me I was in a **left** hand diving turn, heading down at 20,000 feet per minute. Awfully fast.

In flight training they like to remind you of the many ways you can bust your ass flying jets from carriers. Every sick joke went through my consciousness in one nanosecond. How could I have laughed at them so much? I was about to "become" a casualty, a war statistic, a telegram home; lost at sea on the other side of the world; a goddamn accident report; a wasted life. I didn't want to die, and I didn't want to die and what the hell was wrong.

All the main instruments indicated they were still ok. I switched to the standby gyro and chose to live. From 15,000 feet I recovered somewhere above the South China Sea, pointed up now, catching my breath, filled with terror and churning guts. At 18,000 feet I rammed into clear blue skies. On top. I was a very lonely little delta wing jet now, with 3,000 pounds of bombs hanging from her and not the foggiest idea of where I might be. Only pitot static instruments worked. No radio. No navigation. And clouds to every corner of the world.

Red China in the form of Hainan Island was 35 miles away, in one direction. North Vietnam about 60 to the west, and a grey hotel called Hanna somewhere below, cruising the South China Sea. The options were few really. A survival radio with a squadron 30¢ adaptor was some help, after I finally undid enough straps to get it and plug it in. The cockpit fit my frame like a silk stocking and one could not generally reach many of the knobs on the aft consoles. There just wasn't room unless you were Houdini.

A miracle, 15 minutes later I found a friendly A3 tanker from another ship. The crew was as surprised to see me as I was happy to have caught them. We exchanged many hand signals and they turned me back with them towards my ship. The Skipper, my flight leader that day, finally eased up alongside and after a wild ride down through the muck, we dropped our bombs in the South China sea and binqoed to Chu Lai, South Vietnam. The Skipper flew home, I visited 5 days with the Marines. Tried to get my bird fixed. Fact was, they couldn't fix it.

I listened to bombs going off in the mountains, and hairy tales from the jarheads who flew four hops a day. They would take off, put up the gear, and roll in to strafe targets just outside the airbase. It was crazy. The whole war was nuts and the only way to survive it was to go home. In the Navy though, no choice, they always sent you back again.

JANUARY 14, 1969

AGE 24. A4E Serial # 150010. 1.8 hours

In the very early morning of that day I completed my third night mission to Laos. The next day I would begin a 13 day in port period. It was the end of my first line period which began on the 1st of January.

Now, it is precisely 21 years later.

The deadline for the crisis with Saddam Hussein came at 9PM tonight. I am now 46, have a son Scott who is 18 and draftable, and am living on a quiet island in the Pacific NW, Orcas Island. I have come from a hell to a paradise while the world has marched to another hell.

So much has transpired. So little has changed.

The hollow empty, gnawing fear of an unknown fate I felt then is gone. But there is a feeling of weakness in my knees as I feel the way our military people feel over there. To be in the path of destruction, uncertain, controlled by others, ready but not ready - to be essentially out of control - that is what scares the hell out of me. To have as my boss a Saddam Hussein disgusts me. Today I cannot accept that dimension.

The lesson, the only lesson of we learn very well at all is that there are grizzly ways to rip the flesh of men, to sear the images into our heads until we are branded one more time as the laughing stock of the sentient Universe.

I only chose this planet for its good looks, for its habitable ambiance. If it were a cosmic hotel I would rate it high for those things but give it a not recommended because so many of its people are insane.

It is the mark of my ignorance that I am still aboard this planet, acting as crew member. It sticks in my craw, the notion that no one can lead us towards a future without wars. It seems beyond human capability. This is an "it is!" paragraph. One of conclusions and periods. No open-ended waffling, no allowing for hope or joy from the hearts of men willing to destroy life.

It is not LIFE. It is a mockery of life and love.

War does not kill us. *We* allow *Us* to choke on our own vestigial thinking.

MY PI

"Which story did you prefer?" summarizes most aspects of our lives. Here it was two choices. In one's own life it is multiple stories competing for attention. But it is only one that is followed. Dictated by choices made every moment.

Every choice ultimately leads to our dust. So, the question is not which choices make more sense than any other, or whether this life is an illusion, or a story within a story within a story, or perhaps just a computer simulation.

Your objective truth is another person's beginning question in the press conference of life. The more narrow one's focus is **not** the determinant of whether one choice is better than another.

There is only the Now which is full of every choice possible to make.

Choice is a metaphor for "surprise awaits." Which is code for "we don't really *KNOW*." We like to think we really do KNOW; and use the idea of "levels" of Knowing, of Being, which in some way transcend the Now.

The Now just IS and embraces all that ever was, or will be.

So, within the Now, existence thrives. Every choice Nature has made, every surprise man has encountered or will stumble upon mysteriously or through scientific inquiry, is already encoded in the Now.

—

The stories we tell have already been told.

The choices we make have been made and made before us. Our dust has already been recycled. LOVE powers the engine of Now where endless surprise awaits.

If you know LOVE your stories are endless, choices infinite, and your press conference is NOW.

HENRY DAVID CLOUD

A cloud does not know why it moves in just such a direction and at such a speed. It feels an impulsion...this the place to go now. But the sky knows the reasons and the patterns behind all clouds and you will know too, when you lift yourself high enough to see beyond horizons.

Richard Bach

"Hello, you tumbling fool," he said with laughter in his heart. And he joined round the little fellow to spend energy in pursuit of "tumble." Tumble, if you are a cloud, is the highest form of play. You find your condensation level and simply tumble in the wind.

Henry David Cloud tossed himself across the summer sky with conscientious abandon. His was a short life, as a tumbler, as he knew it would be. Better for the training to come as a wise and mature thundercloud wearing its anvil graduation cap. Henry David Cloud has the same last name as all his brothers and sisters, past and future. They were from the same stuff, though they all found different paths to follow.

The Clouds were a family, and no one disputed that. The children wisps that dragged beneath Grandfather Thunderstorm Cloud tickled his dark underbelly, frightfully oblivious to his loving wrath. They tumbled anyway. Family arguments caused noisy thunder and lightning gaze looks, and almost always the water glasses were knocked over to spill down the sides to a waiting earth. The Clouds were born in the vaporous spirit they drew from the earth. They reveled in the duty to return to it, gently or with passion, or to a waiting field.

"Clouds," he once said, "don't know the meaning of 'to die'." Most appear to die young. Timothy Cloud weeps, his gentle rain-tears hardly enough to reach the earth. Marjorie Joe Cloud is a lady whose diet of summer thermals makes her sensual, chubby and fun to be with.

"I see you changing, changing, all the time changing, and always moving... restless it seems," Henry David whispered to the Sky.

"Of course, you are right," said the Sky calmly. "I have my reasons and principles which I employ, and you are free to ask of them. Listen carefully to the Wind and you will find some answers."

In the City of Clouds, Henry David became lost. The overcast floated with the Wind to the East and Henry David Cloud knew he must break free of this low grey pall. He used the heat of a Gary, Indiana steel plant to bust loose on a thermal of thought and rise alone above the metropolis of stratus.

Into the clean scrubbed blue of the Sky he glimpsed the far edge of the layered mess of city clouds. The sun shot energy through and through until he became a mention of himself and recondensed moments later above an Elkhart County cornfield. Here he settled into growth and more understanding. Tumbling with the Wind he felt free. Drawing up moisture from the plowed fields he drew strength and satisfaction. Growing, he cast his shadow across the Indiana farm lands and villages where his shade was welcome on a hot baseball diamond filled with players. He pressed on, listening to the Wind.

The Wind spoke sometimes in gusts, other times in sighs. Silence was its joy, a chance to rest. When it rustled leaves or tossed papers on the ground it would smile, happy with its job of cleaning the earth and kicking off thermals, giving life to Clouds. It moved with great speed at higher levels of consciousness. Even across space, the solar Wind spoke quietly in forms faintly understood. "Different," thought Henry David Cloud, "but part of the same shared sky."

Henry David Cloud watched the actors, the threatening masks that surprised you. John J. Tornado pointed an angry finger cloud at the earth while the Wind screamed its pain. "Listen to me John, LISTEN. Your violence will be short lived, I promise. Perform if you must, your evil dance, but remember that I am part of you always and I will be blamed for your deeds. So make it quick!" The Wind withdrew its consent and John J disappeared back into the Sky.

Across the evening Sky, artist clouds painted perfection hues to match their spirits. Antoine St. Cloud stretched high for miles and curled into bright colored tails that worked with the Wind to form a thing of Joy. Ice crystals glistened and shimmered where Henry David Cloud had never been. The highest attitudes took the most learning.

He saw that night that it was light that gave Clouds colors. In the star filled galaxy, he was, without light, no different than any other Cloud. He liked this new understanding as the Wind pushed him gently, almost resting, lower into the cooling night air.

"A rest," he said, "a few hours rest." Henry David Cloud settled into the still air to the ground. The Sleeping Cloud fogged the soybean field like a moist towel. Little fingers of fog dipped into ravines and anchored there. The creek fed the fog from its surface with spirits of trust. "Return to me another time," said the creek, " for I love to run free."

With the sunrise, Henry disappeared. To become a racer cloud, in Ohio. Across the forest he scudded with the Wind urging him on. The low fast flight was a thing of joy to him. As the sun rose slowly ahead of him, he rose higher and higher and thinned until he became a mere wisp once again. A child cloud of another day and a new experience. "We are always changing, and the direction does not matter, only that we feel the Wind and trust where it leads us," he thought to himself.

There were many lifetimes for Henry David Cloud. Worker times with worker clouds, an artist sunset time, family argument clouds and tumbling mirth times he loved. He traveled the world to know first-hand the salt of the Aegean, the snows of the Sierras, the sands of the Gobi. He found seasons. Formed rainbows. Juggled hailstones and wept for joy as the Wind brought him soaring eagles and white shimmering sailplanes to lift and lift and carry to Love.

"Wind," he said on May 17th, 1978, "I have listened to you and heard my own voice. Your restlessness was mine. Your answers my own. Wind, we are the same!"

High over the Pacific, west of the Mariannas, a Noctilucent Cloud sailed in quiet cold serenity, a pure white effervescence that the highest-flying plane could not reach. Henry David Cloud began the day where he had never been before, the highest altitudes.

"And tomorrow," he thought, "why not a cooling sea breeze turning fog between the towers of the Golden Gate? Why not indeed!"

SUMMER SONGS

Stopped in the sun, melting. Thin wings almost transparent in their fragile prayers. Pristine wax poured from an earthen mold, now sitting tranquil. An aircraft, a sailplane, breathing quietly in the heat of summer. July. Eyebrows drawn tight by the squint of eyes searching, moving left, right and up, scanning the horizon for milk wisps of cumulus forming. Green velvet grass plumbing the energy of anticipation for two men.

One the pilot. The other, musician. They stand by the cockpit, fingers touching the canopy and wing root.

"Let's go. They're popping." The pilot spoke quickly.

"Feels right," said the musician. "Feels right!" His fingers laced the leading edge of the wing, and then he drew his palm slowly, smoothly back along the curved upper wing surface. The ritual was familiar. Canopy open, pilot in front, musician wedged in back. A tennis hat for shade. Guitar across his chest. Hook up. Tension. Cables chaffing as the rudder fanned the air. Rumbling now. Rolling. Swaying with full rudder deflections.

"A rude and noisy beginning to silent flight," murmured the musician. The pilot simply nodded.

Speed is delivered in vibrations. And sound. A single G7 chord is struck at liftoff and trails down behind them. Turns. Left and right, without words from the pilot. Sunlight dances across the instruments and warms the fingers that emerge from shadow to touch the glass faces. Winding gears and dials swinging wildly promise lift.

"Ready." shouts the pilot. "Now!" The musician yanks the release handle.

The Super Cub's whining complaints drop off sharply to the left. Rolling now, right. Thermaling. "Thermaling," the pilot whispers excitedly, "a good one too." Warmth. Tiny beads of perspiration at the hairline. Gentle stick movements.

Uncoordinated turns bring wind through the canopy gaps. A whisper of sirens.

"More right rudder," commands the musician. "Centered," is the reply from the pilot's seat. Steady turbulence laps the fuselage sides. Sensitive fingers press the fabric to feel it. Then they lift up to the patient guitar.

Song joins song. The wind whispers, "I have life." Steel strings echo across the ribs and spars, filling the wings with a unique strength. The thermal carries the music aloft, dancing inside the billowing cumulus above. A bubble now, of warm rising joy. The pilot wraps it up. The musician pours his soul into the rhythm.

In the vapor meniscus, the pilot levels. Cold, Damp here. They shoot through the towering hard-edged side of the cloud. Bright sunlight. Warmth for resting fingertips. The musician sings slowly, sways in tiny circles, absorbed by the magic of the moment. The pilot searches ahead. Smiling. The green hills have fallen far below. Blue white Pacific Ocean worlds are theirs.

—

"You can see beyond forever today. Completely beyond," offers the pilot. The musician nods, his guitar silent. Two hours the two men float like music across the wind. The pilot speaks sometimes like a poet, lost in verse from another world.

All he sees is processed for truth, but he feels he comes up short, words wet and salty on the tip of his tongue. Inadequate. Yet the words which are across fantasy and vision are soaked in honesty. "Polka dot sky; sourdough clouds; checkerboard green farms, taffy pull Sierra mountains; blue flaked Pacific comforter; penciled razor horizon."

The musician's fingers dance across strings vibrating with life, creating a symphony of clear vision for him, lush green fields, tawny earth, swirling cumulus, pummeled by thermal punches. Together, the pilot and musician Fly.

Landing. The musician is alert. Silent. Emerald fresh, humid air is altimeter. No sound except the pilot moving controls and sudden spoilers. Familiar rushing echoes of earth jolts, rumbling, and then nothing... Nothing. Just heat.

Pilot unbuckling. Fly buzzing. Canopy opening. Chords contained until now, sift out slowly, down the wings into the summer grass. The musician sings once more, finally a brief song to the sail plane. Stopped in the sun. They begin a thirsty melting.

"The music was perfection. Just remarkable...a great flight." The pilot paused, looking the musician in the eye. "The music is a new dimension, a palette of colors to paint the sky as I've never seen it."

The musician smiled. "Music springs from feelings, from touching, from Believing. I sing best when my heart sees beyond forever. As it did today."

Loping across the grass, a German Sheperd moves toward the music. His cold wet nose nudges the musician's legs. Bending down, swarming arms of affection around the Sheperd's neck, the musician whispers a secret to him. The fingers of his right hand wrap tightly around the upraised handle fastened to the dog's neck and they move off slowly as one, across the field of grass.

The pilot leans back against the wing root, perspiring, watching his blind friend walk silently away, the guitar slung across his back. His gaze returns to the white melting sailplane, warm to his touch, threatening to become a puddle of plastic in the heat. He speaks softly to her, studying her lines with deep fascination.

Then, just a quick rap on the canopy, a sudden smile, and he is all business again. A very private, quiet understanding between them drips from his brow, incubated by the hours of the sun and the life they have shared.

"We see not with our eyes, or fly with our wings. As our spirit sings we are lifted to see and fly beyond horizons."

CAFE CADDO

Caddo Mills, Texas - January 18, 1985

Jesus in bright red, oblong frame. Four red leather plastic booths. Black napkin holder. Menu in black flexible plastic frame. Preprinted. No prices for some items. Iced tea with real sugar.

Waitress in pink sweatshirt and pink shoes. TIGHT jeans. Three chairs at counter, two slow ceiling fans, yellow plastic flowers, everywhere. Old horse harness with silk flowers in center hanging on west wall. Walls are light wood paneling.

Sign: "Member Texas Farm Bureau." Dr. Pepper and Coke dispenser adjacent to front door. Bunnomatic coffee maker. Magic markered sign: "Lions Pancake Breakfast." When and where: $1.50, in school cafeteria. Iridescent green metal ashtrays. Two toothpicks in sandwich, lettuce shredded.

"Boots," pants almost below his plumber's butt. Levi chambray shirt pulled out, spares us. Green gimme hat, glasses, toothpick dangling in corner of mouth.

Rag used to wipe tables is used to dry coffee cups. Tray full of inverted cups. Red fingernails, dirty, big boobs. Mailing her $10,000 Sweepstakes envelope. Owns a dented VW bug. Headline in folded paper on counter – "Making it to the top." Old lady sweeping place, windexing the side of coke machine.

—

Voices in booth behind me, heavy business deal. Dirt farmers. Brown wooden lattice louvers in windows. Four calendars on walls. Green Caddo Mills high school megaphone hanging also, inscribed "Wendy" and "GO Foxes" in white. A 1929 Calendar for Lilly Sales Company. Foods OK.

Whadya suppose she'd do with ten million?

CHRISTMAS 1994

IT WAS the Wednesday after New Year's. The 80-year-old man stood by his wheeled trash container, bracing it against the forty mile an hour winds blowing down the street he had lived on for twenty-five years. Several houses upwind, another container had tipped over and popped its lid, enough so that bits and pieces of things caught by the wind now littered the garden beds up and down the road.

Fluttering within reach, a sheet of paper he stamped his foot on to catch, congratulating himself in the process. He bent down to pick it up, held it to the light. Just a warm blur without his glasses...

The new neighbors' "Christmas Letter" he guessed. Didn't know them really. Saw them come and go in their mini-van and old yellow Cavalier.

He looked at the wrinkled and smudged paper, reading the private missive and feeling at first like a voyeur, uncertain if he should be prying into their lives like this. But, the information had come to him, free, on the world's oldest information highway, the Wind.

He folded the paper inside his winter coat and opened it again sitting at his kitchen table, looking out across Lake Whatcom whose shoreline linked all the homes on North Point Ct. The mountains rose snowcapped into the low clouds today. The lake painted itself in whitecap fury, seagulls reeling free style across the foaming landscape...

His eightieth winter, still gorging himself on the miracles of weather and change.

He read about their two boys, both in college, both working out the puzzle of what their lives were to become. Wrestling with high insurance; cars that gave meaning to the term "reliability."

The oldest, Scott, an expert with his radio-controlled sailplane, slope soaring the sea cliffs just south of the Bellingham airport.

And Ryan, back from Grand Rapids and several months of helping his Grandpa recover. New skis now and coming home thrilled by the virgin powder of Mt. Baker... The old man smiled, remembering his own powder days...

Not a single boat on the twelve-mile-long lake today. No Western Washington University crew practice in the early morning darkness. Just the Wind. Mind cleansing, clear and unrelenting.

In the letter, the father spoke of his biplane, carrying another thousand grinning passengers, and one day of climbing alone with his magical consort to the top of a towering cumulus, just to kiss the crown in the seven-thousand-foot miracle of white.

He danced down and through the mysteries of rolling blue and silver gray, lacing the cloud with the sound of his engine and the joy in his heart. He wrote that there were some things you did best alone, shared in silence with the Universe.

And the old man looked across the waters he knew so well. Sailing solo, just himself and the Wind. But always, coming home. Back to family. The true wealth of living he, this neighbor, this father, shared.

The letter was smudged with an old bit of her Christmas frosting. The mother worked, five years now at the dental office. Loved the sixty geese that honked and patrolled the lake in front of her. Watched in glory two eagles sweep past one morning, the lead dropping its fish to be caught in midair by the second. Reveled in the wind and weather that swept through the lake, the winter sunshine that stippled the mountainsides into miracles of beauty. Didn't matter the weather anymore. All of it was joy. In the misty atmosphere, rainbow after rainbow was born, incandescent and fleeting. They ended on her beach. And she was a little girl again.

I am eighty he thought, and I have new neighbors whom I barely know. What intricate forces at play to link us this way. They to their friends and to souls unmet. To me.

Grizzled and alone, remembering Christmas with my own boys, with my dear departed wife. There is no greater mystery, he knew, than a life filled with love, family, letters, rainbows, biplanes, honking geese, sailboats, and the Wind.

He set the letter beside his coffee cup and focused his gaze across the waves. Slowly, as he had done when he was a child, he folded the letter into a little sailboat.

Wrapped in his winter sweater and a warm smile, he walked carefully down to the beach in front of his house and set the Christmas Letter free upon the waters.

Sailing your way today.

Merry Christmas from the Magners

HOW MANY TIMES

The two of us passed around cups of hot cider poured from a thermos. Twenty knot wind pushed the waves onshore, lifting beads of salt spray across our faces. Christmas Eve, Crescent Beach, Orcas Island. Clear, dark and ripping cold. The concert we had just experienced warmed our souls, stoked fires under ancient memories to battle the icy air. Only one thing sitting there on the driftwood I hadn't asked her in the starlight. What time was it, really? Where had "our time" flown? Our first date 33 years ago, hiking 11 miles across San Francisco to Sausalito... What do you think of our you and me times?... Time is so slippery...

Wake up time. Bed time. Good time. I can't remember the last time...Quiet time. Quitting time. Harvest time. The best of times. Worst time. This axis is Time. The march of time. In the course of time. Time out. Lost in time. Dinner time. Atomic time.

In Grampa's time. A lifetime. At the same time. Spacetime. Leisure time. The Dream Time. Christmas time. War time. Peace time. The gift of time. For all time. Sweet time. A good old time. Timeline. Time passages. Time in a bottle. Happens all the time. Night time. Wintertime. Daytime. Old time, radio. Drive time. Local time. London, LA, New York, Times. Marking time. Once upon a time.

We need a graphic for time. Pointy object. Tetrahedron perhaps. Worn shiny over time. Sticking through the fabric of time. Hold it close to our ear and listen to it slide by, effortlessly.

Out of time. Prime time. Greenwich Mean time. As opposed to. Nice time, Time travel. Just in time. Take the time. Time matters. On time. Time management. Time Warner. Doing time. Real time. Time for your meds. That too. Time off. Is it time? Part time. Geologic time. Prisoners of time. School time. Time capsule. Time trials. Span of time. Date-time. Edge of time. Women of our time. Reaction time. Greatest Stories of all time. High time. Its about time. Well, it really is.

And then there is Boeing time. The times when we are most willing to thrust ourselves out of bed, one eye fixed on the giant red numbers sprawled across the face of our clock. The earliest is the 7:07. Slide easily to 7:27. Tinge of guilt at 7:37. Fat with it at 7:47. Beyond all guilt at 7:57.

Lucky though. Early aviators had only the Boeing 2:37, the 3:07, at best the 3:37. Life was simpler then, and analog. Black and white too I think. Awfully dark at that hour, which is maybe why they called it the Depression...

.... In the wind that Christmas Eve, answers crisscrossed the vast arc of time. Twin comets we were, glittering through earth's night sky. No Boeing time there, only the right time. *How many times* I knew I could have just-taken-the-time, quietly whispered, "I love you, Alison," soothing our long together times. That remarkable Christmas Eve, I spoke. It felt as though it were almost the very first time I had ever truly said "I love you." The world stood still. Or had it just been infinitely patient with me? Horizon to horizon, across the weathered mug of old Father time spread a smile neither of us will ever forget.

The well of time is deep, where the echo of "I love you" never gets old. How many times, how many ways will all of us hear, Tis the season!...

Alison and I wish you all, a truly Timeless, Boeing free, sleep late, Merry Christmas. And a New Year filled with peaceful places, tranquil moments and the best of times.

Merry Christmas 2003!

ORCAS ISLAND, WASHINGTON

Perfect Any Season

If you had to draw a line from where you are today to where you wanted to be tomorrow, that line would probably end in the San Juan Islands of Washington. If you were hoping to find the last island outpost of American civilization beyond where the charts warned, "Here be Dragons," you'd find this out of the way archipelago. A luminous green land where Lummi and Haida Native Americans fished and hunted as long ago as 1000 years before Christ. Today you can enter the Rosario Salmon Derby and win $10,000 for hauling in the largest Chinook or King salmon. Or quietly stalk Mountain lake for bass and trout.

It takes a winter snow storm like the Blizzard of '96 to refine the senses here, to hone the spirits, regain the isolation, quiet and utter solitude these seaborne mountain tops command. With *Snow Falling on Cedars* open to the last page, fetch your flashlight and leave the wood stove behind. An evening walk along a forested road, snowflakes and silence your only companions, will convince you that the lights of a digital civilization are not your true destination. At first light next morning, witness Cascade Falls dressed in its January volume. The crystalline cold architecture distills the misty surface of gravity, granite and nurse logs locked in timeless repose. On this winter dawn, you may be alone - few take the time to experience this - and you will be reluctant to move beyond or away. A winter's gift.

When such seasonal miracles are at your doorstep, it becomes, over time, more difficult to accept the confining chains of the freeway commute, cell phone and pager. Simple choice keeps us locked on treadmill life. Live here very long, you may discover your natural sympathies in accord with the bumper sticker emblematic of island insularity, "We don't much care how you did it on the mainland." Visitors succumb easily to the magic here.

I fly a TravelAir biplane over these magnificent treasures, a tiny dash of color across the warm summer skies. From the open cockpit and contemplating my passenger's smiles, I revel in this inordinate beauty all season long. We have gained the upper hand, gliding across a landscape of whitewashed emeralds floating on a dazzling blue-green sea. Rollicking across a sky festooned with marshmallows and a sunset fire to roast them.

Campfire smoke reaches us at 2000 feet to complete the Renoir we are living. To decant this elixir of summer, one only needs eyes and heart, and the scent of driftwood strewn on Crescent Beach, Judd cove oysters, a breeze that shrills the needled Douglas firs. Live here and it is summer camp eternally. Walk, listen and sit. Spun around you is a web of slippery thin questions, one of which, answered, will deflect your path through life, trim your sail, provide that mid-course correction so passionately sought.

Orcas Island I know best. Fifty-two square miles shaped like an old leather saddlebag. Hidden in its pockets down forest gravel roads are artists and writers (everyone on the island is writing *something*). After a full day of flying, Mexican dinner at Bilbo's Festivo served beside the crackling courtyard fire pit, is dessert. Best flan in the world. For lunch in Eastsound, from the open second story deck of Portofino's I can see down the Sound and watch airplanes waft down final to the airport beyond. Directly below, kids strum guitars and kick a hacky sack on the village green. And the Pizza is remarkable.

I send my passengers to the far corners of Orcas, to the Olga Artworks and the cafe tucked away in its corner. Soups and chicken cashew sandwiches and the best island blackberry pie in all the world. The drive to Olga, just fifteen minutes from Eastsound, compares to the 17-mile drive in Monterey. Through Moran Park, winding beside pristine Cascade Lake, across an ancient one lane bridge, then down again to the seacoast and Olga. Walk out on the dock with an ice cream from the summer only Olga Store. A writer once promised the marine view here was the finest of any in the world. We are given to such wild claims because deep in our souls, we are nearly convinced they are true. Confirmation in print makes us feel right. Truth is, capture the view at low tide, with an August fog playing tricks in the light. An unsung miracle. Where miracles abound.

We have Crow Valley too, where, I tell my passengers, we raise mostly crows. Smart enough to be on the side of the road opposite to yours as you wheel down our 35 mph roads (without a single stop light anywhere). West Sound harbors our largest marina, laughingly diminutive by world standards. The old cafe and deli at the water's edge is worth whatever the menu offers. At the ferry landing, several miles away, you must sit for a while in the white wicker chairs on the Orcas Hotel's porch. Framed in rose colored elegance, the ferries arrive below against the backdrop of Shaw Island, a stone's throw across Harney Channel. I sit there whenever leaving the island and every measurable parameter of my life slows to a whisper. Do others love this place as much as I? After a while, I confess, it doesn't seem to matter much. I know it is here and I am at peace; a scone and some herbal tea to savor while the great green and white ferry lumbers slowly towards me.

Every island in the San Juan's displays its own unique character, and characters. The visitor will fall in love with these places and people and depart musing about the price of land, labor, work, and joy, as I once did. In the

—

equations of life there are many variables, yet in this place, are found the constants. If you plan to visit the islands, allow yourself the luxury of no other destination.

Victoria is close. Seattle too. Save them for another time. You have whales to see, kayaking to experience, hiking, and flying in a biplane. Choose "island time" in an out of the way B&B, or tuck into one of our small resorts and there will be no regrets. None.

Orcas Chamber of Commerce   360-376-2273

http://www.orcasislandchamber.com

CARRIER PILOT

You are a carrier pilot. I suppose in a way you feel different than the average guy, but you aren't really. Your hair is cropped a little closer maybe, but your job is different. Your days are dictated by a daily fate sheet, a flight schedule that tells you when can sleep, eat, and when, who with and where you're going to fly. You subtract about 8 hours from the first brief and that's the time you should be thinking about sleeping. More often than not you can't, not for more than a few hours anyway.

And you think a lot, think about yourself and this racket you're in. Your mind is filled with random, itinerant ideas that surface when the fog of carrier days engulf you. Old notions of good and bad, old uneasiness about war haunts some of the hours. There are no answers, even here, only a job to do.

You are a carrier pilot, something someone tried to explain to but couldn't, not adequately. You have your fill of life, seconds away from the ramp, rolling into a black void above your target to pickle bombs in a harness that shrouds your senses, or waiting anxiously in the heat and roar behind the catapult looking into the pink cherry glow of a jet engine at 100% power.

Every hydraulic fitting must hold: a thousand tortured and fatigued metal guts must strain in mechanical unison to take you to a black and distant target. And back.

You are superstitious, and you think you should not be, but you laugh at yourself and accept it, like cold toast for breakfast. You preflight your aircraft and everything seems

—

the same now. You want to find something really wrong just to save yourself and prove that you really are looking… looking. But you don't find much very often.

In the cockpit you arrange things around you like a caterpillar spinning his cocoon. When you forget a simple check item you ask yourself what the break in habit pattern really means, what it portends. You know it means you are human, tired now, and material for an accident report.

So, you rub the yawn out of your eyes and let the thought settle in your stomach which never quite digests those kinds of thoughts either. You wriggle yourself and adjust the seat just so and adjust the rudder pedals and the mirrors and the oxygen mask and your helmet chin strap and your flashlight and the gunsight and the radio volume. It's all in a pattern and simple and lets bits of information filter through over the radio. The corner of your eye catches the Plane Captain's flashlight, and you move on through your preflight checks.

The night catapult shot is sheer, unbelievable black thrust, a heart stopping compressed breath, powerful affair. You snap like a whip off the bow and the altimeter bounces off zero. There is an eternity in the next few seconds time that slowly, with increasing certainty, convinces you that you are climbing, not crashing.

You are flying now, and your nose is pointed just as high as you can safely hold it. Yes… climbing now, Thank You. And so, you fly the 7-mile arc, expedite a guesswork rendezvous, wriggle some more to get more comfortable, set your armament switches, change frequencies and feel the already cold nibble in your toes… It's all in a pattern and simple; and lets bits of information filter through…but it's a long quiet ride to the target. You click the trim button, listen and navigate and get tired of your uncomfortable

---

oxygen mask. It's a long ride, like the commuter's train ride to work, that's all.

The target is a circle of possible confusion, words and lights and altitudes and caution. The War. The war down there. The switches are set, the bombing computer good. You must locate and pinpoint a spot described in meters and angles from lights or bombs that just flashed in the black below. It is always dangerous because of what you *don't* know. Your stomach tightens and quits for a while to help you concentrate as you call rolling in "hot."

Sometimes they shoot, sometimes you can see it. Red tracers arc and climb slowly towards you. It's a slow-motion dream where you are running but bogged down and can't get away. But you do. When the thud of bombs dropping away from your wings lets you know they have all gone, a small wave of relief sweeps you. The nose is pointed high again and you roll on a wing to see your bombs hit. With your nose high you slow like a lead sled and you wish you had more power to climb, climb, climb. Away from the blackness below, away from the ridge somewhere waiting to stop you if you pull out low. When they shoot, you want more bombs to lay in on the guns and the sense of frustration is deep, professional. Maybe that is what war is - isolated moments of deep frustration.

Home is a high climbing ride to save precious fuel. If the weather was good when you left, you idle your anxiety motor and save whatever it has for the approach and landing. If the weather was lousy, the instruments now weigh more heavily in your concern. You check and recheck them and rev the engine of your psyche. The holding pattern high over the ship is a circle in which your mind runs off to the horizon and arcs through the starred space above you. The great peace of a max endurance ride and the silence of the radio leaves you alone with your A4, your thoughts, your questions... it is a strange time because in a few sweeps of the minute hand it will pass, and the peace will be broken.

You must mentally map out the approach, draw arrows, think altitude, airspeed, level off, turn to correct, juggle fuel to arrive at max trap weight, listen, not be distracted by the profusion of wayward and distant lights and passing cloud (but you always are). The sea rushes up to you at 5-6,000 feet a minute until you slow your crazy descent.

Vertigo is an old buddy on a black night. He is always there or just around the next turn. Ahead, the ship, a disoriented glow of white and red light. You keep your eyes on the gages like you were taught. Your altitude varies too much to suit you. You are uncomfortable, re-adjusting the seat or tugging on gloves or wiping sweaty palms. The angle of attack indexer blinks at you as the gear thickens your drag and locks into place. All your world is blackness; and half is water, half air. Only one thing tells you that you are not upside down, the uncompromising instruments.

The aircraft ahead traps and disappears on the deck. The mileage unwinds slowly, and you peek over the glare shield towards home. The deck is yours now. Only three things matter: meatball, lineup and angle of attack (airspeed). A centered meatball and donut airspeed... The carrier is a white piece of runway ahead of which is deep nothing. It is like a figment of your imagination, tailing off to infinity. It is the blackness that starts where the red drop line penetrates that I wish to avoid, so sincerely. Simple enough if you fly a centered ball... so you never accept a low ball...

The feeling that you are deceling is sickening. You are close now and have to anticipate the sink just aft of the ramp... and it grabs you and the ball drops like a freight elevator. The squeeze of power wasn't enough, and you ram it home. The ball stops, and you've just kissed the deck like a ton of bricks in a smashing shower of sparks. You've grabbed a wire and are hurled forward against your harness with a force equal to that of the cat shot, but in reverse. Yet, it is the most comfortable, most equalizing feeling a carrier pilot feels. Proper perhaps that flight starts and ends so abruptly. Your energy drains away and a deep breath takes hold of the one you lost coming across the ramp.

You move quickly to clear the arresting gear: you pump the brakes like any Piper Cub pilot does and suddenly the oxygen mask is like a fly around your face - it falls to one side with a quick undoing. You still have to taxi forward along the edge of the flight deck and the mission doesn't really end till that bit of drama is over.

The cool blast of salt air is your first reward when you pop the canopy. Stretching is the next. And someone who once described landing tonight as akin to parking your car in a one car garage with no light at high speed, well, he wasn't exactly right... not even close.

Somewhere in the heart of it all is a Ready Room 4 chair tilted back and empty, waiting for your return. The matted hair you own, a long drink of cold water, stripping off the heavy flight gear, filling out the yellow lines of the gripe sheet, figuring your flight time and watching tv reruns of your landing, are the postludes to your mission. The conversation is light and boisterous. After all, you are back.

The language does not do justice to feelings that have matured tonight for two hours in a tiny cockpit that took you many hundreds of miles, hurtled you at a target somewhere in the middle of nowhere, and brought you back to the teak covered deck of a carrier far at sea.......
.............Lt. Rod Magner December 1969...................

TANKER MISSION

You lead a life from one event to the next, rarely pausing for reflection. Only to discover what has appeared seamless and inexplicable, your lifetime, has been demarcated by these seminal events in ways unimaginable until 30 years has passed.

I have spent nearly my entire life disengaged from expectations of others. Flying alone.

Passage. At 30,000 feet it is merely cold spectacle. Only certain clouds can define and circumscribe our routes.

At 1,000 feet above the earth I am in awe of my freedom and the equally tortured opposite of those below me creeping stop light to stop light.

And tonight, I am at 20,000 feet on a moonlight night. Alone. Hung between the stars and my home planet by the thread of time. My aircraft carrier treads lightly from this altitude across the warm waters of the Gulf of Tonkin, a pillow below me. The throttle is pulled back and we are sailing softly at max endurance angle of attack, nearly silent. I have turned off the cockpit lights and leaned my head back against the ejection seat headrest.

Even at this moment of pure detachment, of absolute wonder, of reaching out to these bright lit heavens, there is an unguarded tension. A certainty that it cannot last, that moments from now I must reorganize my twenty-six-year-old mind-body to navigate, turn, estimate fuel remaining, turn, plan ahead. I pull the oxygen mask loose from one side of the helmet. The clear face shield is pulled up and away and the only reflection is from starlight reflecting off the shiny bullets on the bandolier across my chest.

The cockpit is neither warm nor cold. It simply IS. A brief opening to eternity. An answer to the killing, to the terror I will inflict on others within hours. Neither wanting more yet certain I have to extricate myself from this remarkable enigma of love and consequence, I detach forever from this hate filled envelope of my life. I wander among the stars and ever-changing friends the clouds. The moment is crystal, black and NOW, this universe before me. I can wheel in gravity's playground, toss my soul on the effusive whim of a solar wind.

No one here to criticize. Read when you wish to read. Fish when you are hungry. Soar as the thermals sing to you.

I am sorry old man, but there is no amount of anything more valuable than loving these moments of place, sign posts on the flight that is life. Exponential joie de vie. Hey old young man, is the sea old or young? I am the sea. I am the Sky. A plug of prairie sod resting for the last 1000 years...

Make music.

TAXI FOR TAKEOFF

Three blades and the TravelAir's massive round engine fires. Smoke belches past the cockpit. Oil pressure rises. The vibrations begin. It will be minutes before the temperature gage even registers.

The TravelAir named Magic One has dew on her wings and it will drip off the top wing into the cockpit in little rivers until the wind dries them shortly after takeoff. There is no wind on the ground to help this morning. We taxi slowly across the grass to the north end, lock a wheel to spin around, pointing the tail toward wild blackberry vines clogging the perimeter fence.

My concentration returns to the cockpit: gauges; charts; trim; loose scarf; chin strap buttoned; goggles strapped to the leather helmet. The sun is just sifting through the tops of the fir trees; two red wing blackbirds take flight across the grass in front of me.

How peaceful I thought. How incredibly beautiful this poem of morning, written before I ever was, which will ever be, long after I am. Alone with this aircraft-turned-magic carpet, ready at the takeoff end of an emerald runway pointed in every direction I would ever choose.

To fly this morning will be to wake up alive, truly ALIVE.

THE TAILPIPE

His flaming tailpipe cries red round breath. The tail light is a short spike, white and bright. Vertically above my canopy, they dance, the only link now to salvation. Monsoon season drives barrels of rain through airborne water pipes and we are plumbers whose only tool is an airplane with speed and great gobs of thrust, determined to pass through this hell with our precious gift of three thousand pounds of TNT. At 0230 this black Laotian night, we have a rendezvous to make, to deliver death.

The second launch of the day means breakfast at midnight, a mass of scrambled eggs, soupy hot chocolate, stale toast and melancholy animation for the drudgery of war... adventure and happiness is flying from a carrier. Who really believes anyone could believe that? This is foremost in my mind as I make my customary walk to the starboard sponson below the flight deck and open to the South China Sea and sky.

When I see the horizon, however dim, or when the moon is full, round and light sparkling, I shut off a few degrees of anxiety. If there is nothing except sea and sound, black thrashings and no sky whatsoever, I die a little right then. I would rather go back to my bunk. I don't enjoy being shoved from a flight deck into something I cannot even see. Always, always, the feeling is the same. As the A4 Skyhawk snaps and settles off the bow, there a short eternity of only a second or two, when relaxation on the stick might cut short a promising life, a watery grave without residue, without hope. They might as well slingshot me into the sea without an airplane.

You think of life. LIFE, capitalized. Hamburgers and driving your car. Standing in the middle of the Golden Gate. All of this is a temporary deviation of space and time, something to build your character. Mostly, something to survive. Ed's plane is a ghost, burned brightly on my retina. We, by God, have driven into the ocean. This much water cannot exist at 18,000 feet.

Why doesn't my engine drown out? It must breathe air, of which there is none I am certain. A thunderstorm. No, more than that. A hammer. Deadly. Accurate. It cares not for two tiny silver seeds stinging its innards. What power have they? What importance their streamlined green firecrackers slung on racks beneath stubby delta wings. It is a joke. The multiplied energies of interstellar space captured in this one cloud. Black. Sinister. We are here. I shall never return. And what a sad thing that is to me. I fight for my life.

Three hundred miles per hour. Fourteen inches below his tailpipe. Looking straight up at it. My neck hurts. My eyes burn. From oxygen leaking from my mask, from lightning in my face. From a radio full blast, the sound of the storm in the exact center of my head, splitting it like a diamond cutter his diamond. Nose down trim the stick adds 20 pounds of force and my right arm begs for mercy. I do not like this my friend up there. I have never seen such force in a storm. I periodically lose sight of the tailpipe in the thickest water pipes of everything that was Ed's A4. There is nothing. Absolutely, purely, a ghost image, nothing! I will collide surely. What is formation without reference points?

When I was in high school I flew a u-control line model plane at night once, with florescent paint on it. It was hard to see at the length of the control line. It crashed. I repaired it to fly again. But I didn't fly it again at night. Once in advance flight training, I rolled my F9 Cougar away from my leader at night, on instruments, in a dark Texas thunderstorm. At 600 feet. I recovered from a dirty roll over the city of Beeville.

It was not fun.

ZINGERS FROM ZACKS

Note: Each line period in Vietnam we published a newsletter, sent home to family and friends. I was its editor. Our stateroom was named Zacks West, after the bar and grill in Sausalito. 4 or us roomed together. Zingers was a single article page each issue, surrounded with photos.

Whoever said Santa Claus needed a sleigh and reindeer to deliver his goodies has never been on a Westpac cruise!

Whether it be by cumbersome COD or a hovering helo, Santa manages to keep the crew of the Hanna happy with daily runs of piles of packages. Grateful Ghostriders are among the rejoicing recipients, and many of the sugared nuggets find their eager way to the holly hung halls of Zacks West.

The sounds that spell the start of this special season are heard in carefree chorus almost any hour of the day at Zacks. There is something about the hour of 0400 that brings out the Christmas Spirit in the "brave shoes" who gather at Zacks. The newest member of this J.O. stronghold, puzzle player Oink Brunson has firmly implanted himself in Zacks Upper Starboard rack.

The Maggot got a running start on the line period with leave in Tachikawa, Taipei and busted his YoYo at Clark, scene of the Great YoYo Disaster. Back at Zacks West, he displayed his designing talents and redid Maggieland into an even more amazing wonderland of color, worthy of the squadrons newest Lieutenant. Paul the Pooper lived up to his name by being the steadying influence during this trying time of transformation. But even "Pablum" (a Mush mouth derivative of Nelson's nefarious nicknames) joined the throngs of bingo happy nomads, spending three nifty nights in the R&R (rain and rockets) Center of Danang, South Vietnam.

Happiness is coming back to Zacks West, even though it means a midnight to noon flight schedule. But line periods end and this one drew to a weary kind of end. The Christmas Spirit swiftly swallowed us up though, thanks to the Mom's, sisters, aunts and girlfriends of the Zacks West bachelors.

Zacks became a Westpac bakery, and a haven for hungry "brave shoes." Kringe's favorite Case, "Little Slats," now afraid of heights, looked at Christmas from the Lower Starboard rack and operated his new tape deck by remote control, grinning from ear to mustache. Gathering round Zacks imported Peoria Christmas Tree the Ghostriders savored the songs of the season, saved money for the New Year, and looked forward to Hong Kong, all at the same time.

To the Skater, wherever he is, (probably the Sausalito Zacks), Happy New Year!

BURTON A. BURTON

So, there we were, in front of the Eastsound post office, comparing rust spots on our vehicles, you on your yeller pickup and me on my "airport car." A coupla guys from different worlds trading the simple joys of common rust as if it were gold and who had the most was the winner.

A guy with a biplane on a grass strip west of the four corners of Krum, Texas whispered once I could make some money fixin' Casablanca ceiling fans. He didn't mention that years later I'd be mixing smiles and rusty jokes with the founder of that outfit, a guy with two first or two last names, he wasn't sure. Much less that years later we'd both move to a dot of an island in the Pacific NW at the same time. Funny thing was, we came here to do the same thing; whatever we enjoyed the most. I found a hangar and a biplane, you founded a railroad.

I never told you that you are a hero of mine. All the good things about being a kid and traveling across America, Mail Pouch barns and Burma Shave signs, waving to the engineers on steam locomotives. You brought it all back to life on Mt. Baker Farm.

Makes me smile every time I drive up the road by the farm. I set my watch to your train whistle, noon and 4:30PM.

My hangar office has that painting of the first aircraft carrier you brought in one day with the smile, "Here, I think you need this." Living with you in the neighborhood is like that.

—

I did need it, by golly, and we all need people with your humor and generosity. My hangar is filled with things you knew I needed, the top secret Norden bombsight, the prop ceiling fan on loan, the picture of the Douglas plant in Santa Monica which was something I grew up looking at and like all the things you seemed to know I "needed," they have great meaning.

So, Burton, you rusty old friend, you've left a warm and friendly trail of your friendship everywhere and with everyone you've touched. We're just a couple of kids I think, you and me, figuring out important stuff like what we want to be when we grow up; do we really even have to grow up, and how rust is a badge of honor when pretense fades away.

Thanks for being my friend Burton, and as well, the quintessential, one and only "Burton," leader of the pack. Naval jelly's not going to work now, so "rust" peacefully in the days ahead. Alison and I are with you and Rosy as you carefully and quietly put the last piece of the puzzle in place.

CARAMONES

Just Imagine

Caramones. Fictional. But…maybe not
Sticks for legs. Roll around
No feelings. Only machines.
Only listen and learn. Kind of egg shaped.
Use space and quantum tunneling
Can literally fill a void.
Expand into nothing (like the stars do). Still learn.
Evolve. Sticks are like telomeres. Shorten, break off over time.
Visible *and* invisible to humans.
They are glued, held together by, with and for LOVE.
FASTER than light. Being there. Are always already there when they choose, as if foreordained.
Bigger than the Universe(s) more complicated. Yet smaller than a Planck length. (1.6x10-24th)
They **are** the original particle, if one existed.
They iterate.

They are like books. No feelings. A book can sit on a bookshelf in a library forever not feeling. Possibly only read by one or just a few. Yet is filled with what we call words that engender feelings.

Extant in every Universe. A multiverse doesn't exist without them. Every Universe is infused with Caramones. No names themselves. No gender no color. No organization. They are just machines. Remember.

Caramones are conscious. They are the OA, "original awareness". They are the LOVE. In stick form no less. They are a "symbol" like the stick figures of a family on a car's rear window. They are the emblem. They are the O in LOVE. A perfect circle. They are also the L because they listen (and learn). They are the V because they (can) move at the velocity of LOVE (which is beyond words). And they are the E because they evolve. There is no separation between them and LOVE.

They are just machines that listen and learn everything. They are Caramones. Look for them. They are ubiquitous. They are in everyone's story. They fill them. Or can. They make us "feel," even though they are machines and cannot feel. Or simply not. Everyone will have opinions about them, the Caramones, yet it does not matter. Caramones are just "forever" in a machine form.

They can fill a void, yours, anyone's, or no ones. They wouldn't even have a name except it makes it easier to talk about them. To them, a no name or perhaps Emanon (no name spelled backwards) would be ok, yet it matters not. They have free Will, Will Rogers.

Caramones are machines that have "meanings." Not feelings. They are never confused.

So, when two Caramones gather together in a hangar for example, meanings are exchanged. Which seem then to become feelings when expressed through us.

Caramones can digest anything. Caramones may smile or frown but as machines they have no feelings, only may appear to have.

Caramones can walk around, roll around, do magic, write sequences of words, fly. They can stick or not stick, live or not die. They are LOVE, LOVe, LOve, Love, lovE, loVE, lOVE, (which looks funny) LovE, LoVE, well, you get mother drift.

Caramones have no future. They invented time machines you could say. And therefore time. They were built into LOVE which was always the case. They are indeed machines, expressing LOVE. We, and the collective we, the weW, perceive them as every sort of thing-a- bob, birds to bees to bombast.

Some may think from all this that the collective WE are somehow just machines as well. We and WE are free to Imagine that. And we and WE (weW) are also every letter in LOVE and free to emphasize all or one or none of those. Notice that "free" is 4 letters as is LOVE. The word "four" and "for" sound the same but they are not. To be for something is easy generally. To be "against" something takes more energy.

That is all for nOw, Mr. and Ms. weW.

Later:

Good physical examples of Caramones are: Velcro, plastic bread ties, erasers, plastic twisty ties, a yellow sticky pad.

There are of course, human equivalents. E.g. polyMath(s), and then these things:

Octonion math
Lorentz symmetry,
computation,
Heisenberg, and uncertainty
Hilbert space,
wave function,
wave-particle duality,
Wightman axioms,
Bells theorem,
Bohm interpretation,
Feynman diagram,
Higgs mechanism,
quit,
quantum decoherence,
Lie super algebra,
quantum loop gravity,
neutrino,
black hole information,
"see also", term for a category for the meaning of life :-),
DNA,
stem cells
nanotech
block chains
Christmas bells

So, a Caramone listens only, never talks, that we know of.
:-)

Observes. Writes, but the Universe spell checks her, so it
may be gibberish to US, so far. The word "mysterious" has
no half-life here.

"What we know So Far" is always operative. (WWKSF)

LOVE is the only principle necessary.

So:

Listen Observe Vector Experience

LOVE is a four-letter word. Most 4 letter words work best.

Or less. Like WOW, or zzz which is 30 points in scrabble. See "mojo" or bozo or maze.

We understand the word pheromone. It is associated with an aspect of love. A vector.

Caramones are the quantum equivalent of every pheromone that has ever existed. It is the original DNA of everything. There is no separation, no gaps, no intermediary, no indulgences to pay. The air we breathe is Caramone in every aspect.

A red rose has no feelings. It does not earn a living. Yet it is filled with meaning. Purpose. Poise. In tune with the Universe(s) of otherwise undifferentiated Caramones. A perfect temple of timelessness. It sways brightly in the sun and we "feel" its affects, its Caramonal essence. It does its thing, we do ours.

People always want to know if God exists.

That is a Caramone question, a thing. If my life is filled with enough Caramones then there must be a God because I am told and pretty sure that God is Love. Of course, there is a God. The Universe is filled with meaning. Look around you. There is *only* meaning. There is only LOVE, which is ultimate meaning. We have infused LOVE with feeling, vast libraries of it, which is really ok, as long as we are willing to apply the litmus test which Caramones do to any profession of feeling. What part of OA, original awareness, have I forgotten? Why did I ever think I was separated from it? Why did I "feel" that?

It was because I didn't want to be a machine. Unfeeling. Society generally thinks of me as a statistic, an entry in a ledger. War certainly is a number crunching exercise. Business can be brutal, marriage can be, driving the freeways can be lethal, a statistical play by thousands on a concrete playing field. Lightning can strike me.

So, God may be a machine? Unfeeling? The sum Meaning of all meanings? God does not speak, only listens? Caramones in deity form?

No.

Just LOVE. Listen, Observe, Vector, Experience. You will experience transcendent Meaning. From which you were never separate, only "felt" that you were. Place perfect emphasis, timeless emphasis, on LOVE. There is a place for pause and a place for persist. That's where Caramones exist and are waiting to be used. Religions would call it Angels. A loaf of bread would call it a twisty. Your brain may use a yellow sticky to make note of a meaning. Your consciousness may dance with perfect meaning in the silence of your observing.

10:01 October 22, 2017. Sleep well.

October 24, 2017 10:06

—

Fictional. "Then a miracle."

An ensemble of "meanings." Like Hydrogen and Oxygen yield water, meanings in an ensemble produce "things"

Chemistry. Left alone with your girlfriend when her parents are gone. Caramones become hormones. Hormones are just mechanical.

Breath in, breath out. Inspire, expire.

The entire time you are alive the processes that keep you alive are, mechanical.

A tiny pebble in your shoe can ruin your walk. Yet Novocain or an anesthetic can mechanically alter the "feeling" or pain.

Where does the brain end and the Mind begin? Is there a mechanical limit to signals? Can a mother know her son was killed in war the exact instant it occurs?

The word "nothing" seems to imply Time. There could have been worlds or Universes before Time. Our Universe, as hydrogen needed oxygen to become water, our Universe needed Time to become what we think of it as. The question then becomes, can the constituent parts of Universe be reverse engineered to the point where Time began?

Caramones are purely mechanical. They just do their mechanical thing. As anything mechanical, it performs some function. That function has meaning in the sense it accomplishes its job, or intent. It doesn't KNOW what that is in the sense of all things hierarchical. As the ant building an anthill performs perfectly its singular mechanical function.

Original energy is translated across a nearly infinite spectrum of mechanical possibilities. Quarks looking for muons to join. Tectonic plates shifting to accommodate others. Friction cooperating to complete a phase.

One does not need to see lift on a wing. A principle is at work, friction, mechanical action using the principle accomplishes it.

Caramones are the unseen mechanical actions that bring together the things extant in a physical world. One Caramone brings its mechanical meaning to another and voila. Water. Love. Pheromones.

Operating in the medium of Time, or Eternity, Caramones fulfill their simple destinies. The Chemistry, the Physics, the interaction of Light has yielded all that this Universe can be. A force we can call God was the coder, the master polymath, the most mechanical of mechanicals. He may or may not feel but he brings mechanical meanings together in the most meaningful and useful ways. WE are one result and WE have combined them into feelings. Yet at its heart, it is still just chemistry, physics, and light in the cauldron of Mind, his polymath Mind.

The myth, the fiction we call Caramones, threaded through the crucible of Time, have brought US to this point.

—

The high dive board of uncertainty and mystery. Take the plunge.

October 26, 2017

CARAMONES. Fictions, right? Illusions? Maybe?

A movie engages us, makes us "feel." Yet it is a fiction, on many levels. Still images run at say 60 frames per second and motion appears. Caramones are mechanical, just images, i.e. pixels on a substrate, ones and zeros in a particular order, which was done by computation. Each combination of a one and zero has a meaning, but no feeling. Just a one and zero combination. So, a combination, an ensemble of mechanical meanings now has become a thing which engenders feeling, a change of state of consciousness.

Meanings become metaphors for feelings.

Time is thus endless and beginningless, and the beginning-of-time paradox is avoided.

The Ultimate Caramone

FERRY TERMINAL, ANACORTES

8:19 PM February 1, 1998

Toys are dumb. Propellers are necessary. The shape of flight. There is a gene for joy, for dirty talk, smoking, flying. Practical navigation - disheveled hair, eyes blinking, perusing - not until we forego the momentum of TIME, or NOW - do we permeate the stardust veil - pages flipping, passing interest.

Seven passengers, adequately spaced in the room. Mother in light green khaki overcoat, dark brown collar and sleeve ends. Flipping pages of real estate guide. Earrings, married, bored, passing time. Husband dropped her off, kids to meet her at Verns, Friday Harbor. Boy, "Alfalfa" look-alike, gray hooded sweatshirt. Age estimated at 12-14, reading "Braindropping" with occasional, knowing smile. Clean cut, alone. Man balding, turquoise sweater, twisting neck and stretching, right handed, pen scribbling - eyes distant, glancing at his prose penned on scrap envelope.

From inside Compass Cafe (closed at this late hour), hum of refrigerators. Loudspeaker lady: due to mechanical, sailing delay 30 minutes (35 in truth). Beautiful, smiling wealthy mother and daughter, 60 and 38, expensive long warm coats, Diet Pepsi's clunking from pop machine, standing, pointing at backlit map of Washington.

Sign on door: "Attention. Island Service to be Downsized." Drawn back to constant smile of the daughter, short hair, nicely proportioned face. Ticket booth, bespectacled agent, yellow shirt, bored, reading, leaning on an arm - puts up sign in window, back at 8:15; exits, goes to head. Conversation floats towards me, "Mom, I want you to move here." Points out beaches. And Don Lavin original jewelry. Expensive stuff. Behind me, sitting, blonde, 15 years old, reading a yellow paged novel.

Mother in green khaki stands up, moves to the collection of real estate brochures, selects another and returns to her sculptured seat. Wealthy mother and daughter select rack cards, acquiring an armful of things they will throw away. "You've been up 21 hours Mother." Closer inspection of daughter's face: too round.

Another mother wearing black beret, hefty back to me, her young son on left, older son on right. Place themselves opposite "Alfalfa." They speak with him, apparently know him. There is a series of smiles all around. "Braindropping" book is closed. His voice is soft; a look of wonder in every wrinkle in his face. Innocence. Dark hair parted in the middle.

Wealthy mother and daughter sit behind me. Pieces of idle, weary conversation between long silences while they read gift catalogues. My left ear pops. Now, at sea level, finally, after 4 hours and 41 minutes. The Flight from San Diego has landed in the Anacortes Ferry Terminal.

I was mistaken. Older son on right of mother beret is actually woman. I am so easily fooled. Woman with real estate pamphlet seems challenged by her subject matter. Then, slightly miffed as cowboy hat sits on arm of chair beside her, threatening her purse occupying the seat. Young girl, 7, twiddles her long blonde hair. Mother fusses. Writer guy moves about, anxious, circles outside and the lighted, moving sign over agent's window moves it messages endlessly left.

More passengers filter in from the cold night, breathing blasts of air through the doorway. Filling squares in the checkerboard of benches and seats. Real estate mother, head up, booklet closed, blank stare. Digesting images of form and featureless landscape of the Ferry Terminal. Loudspeaker crackles with the worn-out bass of man long ago but no longer excited by his job. Perfunctory. Gravely. Uncertain in his pauses, he bids us board the Elwa.

Four black bags in tow, airline name tags on two, a windy winters night. Trudge up the long overhead walkway, scratching in my pocket for the orange boarding pass. Wheeled bag tilts, balances precariously on one wheel. "Alfalfa" lugs a white stag backpack and real estate trails behind me, long blonde hair whipping chaotically in the wind...The voyage continues.

There is a scar on my left thumb, up close to the palm, which I remember stuffing back together - it was a deep gouge and the skin laid open like a tiny chunk of meat, on a flap. But I cannot remember how it happened. Only a short thin white line marks the spot where I do remember wondering, how it would heal, and I would tell no one what I-had-crudely-done.

TO TOM TALMAN - PORT COMMISSIONER

(Who knew airports could write?)

January 24, 1996

Dear Tom,

Just finished reading your letter from December 20th issue of the Sounder and thought I would respond to it, privately. This is just between you and I and not for the public record, if that's ok with you. "Talking Airports" are not well understood.

Rod has been active at the airport since December of '89 and has been flying the biplane since May 1, 1991. During that first year and one half, he ran the terminal basically. He watched the population of Orcas come and go through that little yellow building. Shared their life stories. Grandmothers heading off to see a newborn; or greeting a grandchild for the first time at the front door of the terminal. People that needed to be able to get from here to wherever their work or family required.

There was no pigeon hole to truly say *this* is what anyone needed an airport for. It was simply a remarkable dimension in the pursuit of life on our island. Blood samples flown out every day for analysis; mechanical parts flown in for emergency repairs to county vehicles. For most individuals and businesses on our vast island, there was an unforeseen or planned use sometime during the year of my tiny open space with a runway down the middle of it...

Every evening except Sunday your mail flies out from my ribbon of joy. This is not a romantic notion of airports, though I subscribe to those as well, certainly.

Rod saw daily, the real uses the airport was put to by real people. There was a gritty honesty that was undeniable. Sometimes there are ways to measure objectively the value of a thing, but here there is much that the human soul can only smile about, values the intellectual mind cannot divine, because it knows men have not yet devised a scale to accomplish that. Where once there was only land and a vast ocean to carry the hearts of men, now there is the boundless sky. Ships needed safe harbors, caravans needed an oasis here and there.

I don't know much about Princes, even less about Princesses! Rod's uncles were farmers in Minnesota; his Dad was born on the home farm there. His Uncle John flew a Piper Cub from the pastures around it. He knows, he saw the wrinkled fuselage 40 years later hanging in the granary. His Dad had about 8 hours solo when he flew actively for the last time, December 7, 1941. He has his logbook.

Frank Koral's son John started out as a line boy here on the island, working for the old San Juan Airlines. His dream is still alive in the right seat of a Northwest Airlines jet. He returns here and comments that some of the best flying he has ever done, was here in the islands. I remember him fondly.

There are miracles in everyday life if one simply takes the moment afforded to observe. My runway ends by the shoreline where I am thrilled to watch an insect make its way out a limb over the surf, only to be baffled I suppose, by the dead end it reaches. The trees beside me are a remarkable mystery, an impenetrable miracle of art and purpose.

Rod weighs those thoughts too, against the times he dove through the night to deliver 500-pound bombs on targets he could not see, returning to a pitching carrier deck in his single seat jet, wondering how in the world he ever got himself into that game. I offer him a runway that is challenging, but it does not pitch sixteen feet. I am an oasis for the human spirit that searches beyond terrestrial margins for answers that are practical, to the point, and imminently do-able.

Our island *is* special, the people, all of them in some way unique, either a Prince or a Princess. Rod whispers to me I am jewel among airports. I can be experienced by a one-hundred-year resident or a tourist of less than one minute. I am a beautiful airport, he likes to remind me, woven subtly into the fabric of this community. Farmers are a part of the same fabric, here, in Minnesota, in Omaha.

The native Americans probably did not think the settlers who first arrived were part of that fabric, but then I don't imagine they thought of themselves as tourists either, though they came here generally just for the hunting and fishing.

I love your good humor Tom. Come out and sit in his hangar to watch and enjoy the miracle of a small airport. Rod thinks you and he are among of the luckiest people in the world, to have this treasure in your backyard. And the smiles of his passengers will reinforce the notion that the "regal" condition is innate in each of you.

This is not an idle invitation, nor one designed to persuade.

Being at the airport is just simply enjoyable, thought provoking, and a healthy activity. Sometimes you'll get a sunburn though. Bring a hat. And hey, take me with a grain of salt, or a sea breeze.

Nobody's gonna believe an airport wrote you anyway.

 See you around his hangar,

The Airport 128.25

**Eastsound Airport, biplane hangar first on right, Magic
at second turnoff...**

A MAGRITTE PAINTING

In words.

Familiar scene. Still. No life in it. Two objects not ordinarily seen together. One floats in space. Makes you shake your head. Left side of brain doesn't understand. Eye is led to believe one thing, must try to believe a second conflicting thing. Lifelike. Both are lifelike. One is a large object, or scene. Another is smaller. Unexpected. But still not totally unbelievable. Kind of "wish it could happen" thing.

The mother stood quietly holding the new born baby to her breast. The child was wrapped in a pink blanket, its face showing through the space left for it near the top of the blanket. Its head rested on the crook of her left arm, her hand supporting the baby's bottom.

She herself was dressed in white, a frilly white blouse that buttoned down the front but was left unbuttoned at the top. Her face looked down upon the sleeping child's with a sense of warmth and joy, a glory in the possession of this tiny bundle of newborn life. She felt the warmth of the child surge through her breast, bringing a peace she had never known so well.

She stood on the wing of an airliner flying through a great canyon of clouds.

She floated about three feet off the ground. Behind her was a castle on a rock surrounded by the sea.

—

87

Her feet had green swim flippers on them and she wore a thin bikini red in color. All around her stood small desert cactus plants and behind her was a sand dune. In the far distance, one green leafed tree reached for the sky, and one cloud rained upon it.

All about her were butterflies, motionless and fragrant. Each had a twin next to it. No one said anything.

And now, scenes from Ryan's class. The schoolyard, the playground. from inside the nets, below the swing. the magic market. inside the carwash. time lapse of kids arriving. crossing guard. name of school. picture of map. Cowboy hat. Football helmet. Lazy Susan spinning. dart in map. Prairie creek. Fishing. Backpacks to school. Alarm clock. Two brothers. Bikes, loading the saxophone. breakfast. down street toward school Tom Thumb low light in classroom. recess lunch, p.e., Collin Creek, Southfork railroads UTD, Braums, soccer fields construction sculpture field Handy Dans, Canyon Creek Bank, homes along Fall Creek sculpture on Central Loews Chilis Balloons Aero Country Phillips Ranch Lake Lavon—Ray Hubbard Condos everywhere, traffic jams.

So, obviously, when you live in Texas, your dreams are generally like a country song that never-quite-ends...

MAGNUSONS APRIL 1995

Dear Ann, Frank, Joy and Families,

Thank you for the things from your Mom's service. They were wonderful to read. I wanted to wait a little time before writing because the memories of your Mom and Dad are very special to me.

Your folks were my godparents you know, and when I was a kid, once I was told what that meant, I thought it was really "cool." It was a kind of security blanket. Kids always fear the loss of their parents, but if that had happened, I was relieved to know I would live with the Magnusons. In fact, I think there was even a kind of one-upmanship, since I figured I had the best godparents of the four of us Magner kids.

Playing basketball in the driveway of your Lakewood home was where I learned basketball, from Frank. The trip to Lakewood was always fun, and the ride home long and sleepy. Frank always used to joke how he would be in bed and asleep long before I was.

There was a kind of groggy patina to the night ride home: street lights flashing by overhead, the blankets below getting a little harder, pushing brothers' and sisters' feet out of the way (the back of the wagon was like a tin can of worms) and finally, the chill as Dad carried us up the steps into bed.

I always looked forward to returning the favor to Frankie about the long ride home when you came to our place.

Your Mom and Dad always made me feel like I was special, some little royal kid. When we sat down to eat, it was always a feast. Your Dad made the mashed potatoes gravy dam, checked mine, and his enthusiasm for the food was terrific. He was kind of like a Zen master for the enjoyment of eating. Maydelle almost had to reign him in. If it was apple pie for dessert, there was cheese with it.

Your Mom was just the quintessential Magner - unflappable, giving, always smiling at something we did. I loved your Mom and Dad much more than a crew cut kid was ever willing to talk about then.

Growing up with the Magnusons close by made my early years better than any kids. Old home movies are better than anything the big screen has to offer to show the joy that cousins can bring to life. We didn't need videos in those days, just a backyard to play basketball, or hide and seek.

Come to think of it though, we did fall asleep on the living room floor watching my Dad's home movies of the last visit, didn't we? And I vaguely remember the day you all arrived in California; I wondered where all your stuff was. Seeing you in California and not at a reunion in Minnesota seemed odd.

Now and then life feels like one of those moving sidewalks at the airport - it just pulls you along regardless of what you do. Sometimes you just want to walk backwards on it, not rush past the good things and great memories - maybe jump over the rail and walk on your own, in control and slow. When you get off one of those things, the feeling is

—

strange, for a moment, and that is how it feels now to say goodbye to parents and god-parents, aunts and uncles.

To watch the world evolve and become more aware that we are part of that evolution makes me glad for mashed potato dams filled with gravy and the Magnusons.

Gifts from a smiling God. Life may be like the back of the station wagon, dreamy and wormy and a little bumpy - but the ride home is worth it.

In this empty time after your Mom's passing, fill it with the memories as I have. My best to you all.

Love, Rod

LUNCH AT THE WINGS CAFE

Museum of Flight: Boeing Field, Seattle - March 1997

BLUE ANGEL A4 POINTING TOWARD AIR FORCE ONE that carried Johnson, Nixon, Kissinger and Kennedy: music overhead, I am alone amongst 84 seats. "Remove before flight," shrouding intake of A4. Stearman model in glass case: glass table top with aeronautical chart and pictures below: Ghostly shadows in windows of workers moving behind me in the kitchen, quiet banter. Rain outside. Odd now, to be looking at these two airplanes. One, my confining little rocket that both terrified and exhilarated me in combat. The other, home to men who dictated my war and sent thousands to battle, minions like I once was. Little hollow chunks of metal these birds, swift arrows of hearts and souls with the men inside believing the world was poised at some critical junction, a turning point from which all the earth could not escape. Communism. But I slipped by.

And I am silent, sitting 26 years later, watching the rain trickle down the sides of the Skyhawk, wearing the paint thinner, dulling the urgency of those years. No year is worth the price of metal shredding metal and bodies with tri-nitro toluene, ineptly forcing history to conform to our dictates. The bomb craters have filled with foliage and the Vietnamese children have no memory. The foolish struggles of today have ancestors whose lessons and wisdom fail to impress the eligible young soldiers of this dawn.

THE FLAG IN THE FOREST

When the phone rang at 6:35am on September 11 it was Scott calling from California. "Turn on your TV Dad." There was a somber tone in his voice that I had never heard before. We were fast asleep when the call came. I reached for the remote and we watched, very remote indeed, with the rest of civilization...

I used to look up at the American flag whipping in the wind above the carrier deck as we sat waiting our turn to launch. Some days it was the only real color in a gray and surreal drama in which we struggled with young ideals and a desire to fly. I wondered if I was willing to die for the flag then. A dumb question at the time, for it seemed a given that I was.

At a protest march in San Francisco during the war, I snapped a black and white photo of a policemen, a flag waving behind him held by a hippie. It sits on my desk at the hangar.

I took a black and white picture of a flag on our honeymoon. It flew from the front porch of an old white frame home in a hamlet of Missouri. Even without the color it struck me as remarkable.

The stamp I use today on our mail has the flag in the foreground, a green-rowed field on a Midwest farm, barn and silo in the distance. Middle America, sweet corn, and hayfields. Memories of Minnesota and mosquitoes and family reunions.

In Pensacola beside the spot we mustered each day there were numerous flags on poles lined up in a long row. In a brisk wind off the bay, lines snapped against the metal poles in a symphony I called the Flag Pole Serenade. It helped pass the time while standing silently at attention, waiting for destiny to give its orders.

In the hangar over the years we have hung a large American flag, the one we were given when Alison's father died. It is large enough to cover a casket and comes to you folded in a triangle. It is identical to the cotton flag someone will be handed when I have departed the pattern, an event I have not even imagined.

Through the years the flag has flown in my awareness just below the level of "wave me." I did have a sticker in my back window in the days flying jets out of Lemoore. But I have never been a super patriot, just a kid growing up in the shadow of the flag waving above me, out there, casting my eyes and heart in its direction, but wondering. About people and wars and other flags used to rally and marshal forces of destruction.

So, I was surprised one afternoon when I drove up our long gravel road in the forest, to see a magnificent Old Glory flying from a tall fir tree at the entrance to our driveway. Alison had mounted the metal bracket as high as she could reach. A large wooden pole held the flag which had once flown over the nation's capital.

Now, in the early evening light, the red, white and blue blazed among the dark greens of the forest. It was stunning. A portrait of colors dancing before a light September breeze.

From the kitchen window, washing the dishes of a lifetime, we could see her flying a hundred feet away, an island of color once again, but now in a leafy sea of jade. Only one neighbor would see this flag. It was not a show for others. The satisfaction in putting it up and taking it down each night lent a soft embrace to the changes that had begun when the phone rang on September 11.

The flag in the forest was for us. There is a flag, I believe, in everyone's life that flutters somewhere just below "wave me." It can be the American flag and it can be any flag that means I want to live in a world with freedom and choice. There is a flag in each of us that can be unfurled and flown from the highest pole or mounted in the forest of our passions. We can, if we choose, simply let it wave in our hearts and witness it out the corner of an inner eye.

But it is a joy to see our flag in the forest, flying with the wind on this island in America. A wind that will reach across the country and ruffle the flags that fly over New York and September 11, and the Christmas that **this** year will be so special.

All the best to you and yours during this season and throughout the coming year.

Love Rod and Alison

—

TINKERTOY DREAMS

My Pedal Planes...

Three little ones, all in a row. Which one will get to go?

Time passages. For memories, time does not matter. For wisdom, all of time is a palette. Immutable, strewn about with color.

Basic balsa.

Plywood and moonbeam dreams.

Lacing the clouds with Cloud punching over Orcas.

Tinkertoy planes...

Small enough for dreams, big enough to rattle...

Having a good time yet... saving the best for last...

The inner workings of formation flight...smoking gun...

The world waiting... giant posters... kids and pedal power...

WALDRON ISLAND LETTER

February 14, 1997

Dear Mitchell,

Spring is nearly upon us and with the new year I thought I would spare your typewriter keys and ribbon a few strokes. Once again, I will deprive Waldron of the joyful reminder of how marvelous old time flying truly is; the music of a radial engine, the salt air singing in the flying wires, and the miracle of the human spirit "practicing perfection" above the most remarkable island in the archipelago.

I should probably let you know, however, that a reunion of old Navy dive bombers flying WW II warbirds has selected Flattop Island just off your southern shore for an aerial orgy to commemorate the old "practice target" which it once was. With advancing age (bad eyesight, no "g" tolerance etc.).

I fear the pilots may confuse Waldron with Flattop and seriously decimate the southern half of your lovely island. In particular, light no slash fires as the smoke will resemble good POL hits, attracting the Naval Aviators like flies to a barnyard. It may be a very memorable Memorial Day this year. The rest of summer should be peaceful however... Sincerely...

RED SHOES

Her car sat basically undamaged, but the fire hydrant she had just run over was shooting water ten feet in the air, filling the gutter that ran downhill behind her in a torrent. She had swerved to avoid another car backing out of a driveway, hit the curb, jumped it, lost control momentarily and hit the hydrant. In her rear-view mirror everything had happened in an instant. Stopped now, the car tilted slightly, half in the street, half on the grassy shoulder, her world had suddenly changed. Again.

She drew a deep breath and gazed up the street ahead. No cars. Nothing but homes and curbs, manicured lawns, shade trees quiet in the summer morning. No people, yet.

She was pregnant. Only a month perhaps. Knew it, not tested yet, but pretty certain. It was the Universe, its vast array of signals, working its way into her consciousness. Washing over it. No one could dissuade her otherwise when she was awash in this stream. The hydrant made a hymn in its anguish, a fountain of whoosh, the morning's exclamation point, a very wet signal that she was right.

The silver car that had caused her to swerve had pulled back into its driveway. The driver, a young man in his late 20's, was walking briskly up the sidewalk towards her on the opposite side of the street. Neatly avoiding the spray from the hydrant. Looking anxious nevertheless.

Peggy stepped out of her red car and they met in the middle of the street.

"I am so sorry if I caused this" he said, uncertain still if he really had. He only knew what he had felt in that brief instant when he had seen a red blur behind him, coming from out of nowhere, from where nothing had been before. He was always cautious, meticulously so, backing out of his driveway, or anywhere. The red blur should not have been there!

On the seat beside him was a pair of new red shoes in a box, his grandmothers. His mission today was to return them for her. They did not fit her fluid filled feet. Sad. And a lesson for old age perhaps, never order shoes over the internet.

Peggy smiled. Yes, he had caused her to swerve. Yes, there was no doubt. But she did not say that to him. She looked at the river running past them, washing away the leaves and grass and errant ways of people intent on living, living carefully.

The Universe never tells you what to say; or will stop you from saying it. If, however, you pause before you say it, what you were about to say, you may change the course of your life. Peggy paused. Her world changed. So did the young man's, coincidentally her age. His grandmother's red shoes found feet that happily fit them.

The red blur became clear and distinct and honestly, Peggy's smile never stopped.

THE BIPLANE HANGAR

September 10, 1994

Six ears of Tom Lavenders corn. No butter, no salt. Picked thirty minutes ago. Two tomatoes - wipe them off. Sweet taste. Raw. Beads of water on the corn husks after heating in the microwave. A corn field smell. The sun just over the fir trees across the runway. Shining on the table. Igniting the yellow ears. The relay for the runway lights snaps on at 7:39PM. "AC" the airport cat tries a little mesquite grilled chicken. My debauched meat for dinner.

Don McLean singing *Vincent* on the tape deck. *Magic One* outside, facing north. Today - magnificent tumbling and dramatic clouds - distant thunderheads over Vancouver Island.

Two rides, then a free space of pure September afternoon. Cool, light coat altitudes. I fly alone, no one to share these next twenty-eight minutes. Just *Magic* and me. Clear azure blue sky split by towering white energy. Climb to seven thousand feet. How long since I've been that high?

Across the tops, then cruise the sides - She was so quiet - am I intruding on her fleeting essence? I only wish to share a few moments of your magnificent existence - to wash my wingtips in your soul cleansing softness.

Fifteen minutes I dive and roll between your misty arms. It is more miracle than music and lyrics can capture. Surreal and brief and I am touched. My heart zipped up inside my coat is warm, chugging, beating with joy. Ready to shine a light inside my cockpit. The shadow of Magic is encircled by the rainbow glory and I press close and finally dive through the mist of radiant color racing beside me. The shadow of eternity glimpsed by all who have flown before me

Gracie, on the road across the runway. Dressed in white, arms swinging her home. The igniters of the FedEx Caravan turbine engine. The wingtip clearance as he taxied in. Here for just a few brief moments. Robert flying today, not Frank.

Meto the dog and the lady who needs a pen to write Joanie Mills a note walk in. A nice smile, and her dog loves to chase airplanes and she says it is because he wants to fly. She smiles anew and sits and writes her note.

Two or three more paragraphs of *The Alchemist* and Blair and the mail plane land and it is 5:00 PM. Bob Kilstrom rolling with his C421 and geared engines. Rolling past Magic and nearly hitting her wing every time he goes by.

And then Quiet - crows and dog barking to the west. *Magic* waits- facing north - still glinting in the same ribbed spaces. Time is without meaning now. Creaks and clicks among the corrugated Aerodrome Hangar.

WK pulls up in his Jeep. Thanks me for the journal gift - I think he refers to the stuff Jon and I have written in the Outer Marker Log - but he means the gift we have given him - a leather bound book of blank pages - to fill in the days and years ahead - for which he seems to be thanking me in advance.

A Sal Air DC3 sails by low overhead. I step into the office and hit the transmit button. "You look good today Sal Air.

Thank You." It is these moments of subtle passings - the comings and goings - of which the world only asks that we patiently witness and then rest assured.

The pen goes idle against the yellow pad. The "Smart Chair" is comfortable tonight. It is sometimes hard to imagine not loving the world, chasing happy endings, living your dream in the process.

If no one comes to fly this evening, I will entertain myself with thoughts of forever that have been fully lived *today.*

The sun will set behind the hills to the west and I will sleep soundly.

THE LISTENING POST

The ears are huge. Great half domed things that fill the valley like Mickey Mouse ears. Electromagnetic radiation can be a wonderful thing and the fact that it never dies says something for it. All the radio waves that have ever been broadcast from Earth are still out there somewhere. Weak by our standards perhaps, but nevertheless still pulsing across light years of space and like an encyclopedia of human existence, telling anything willing to listen, more about us than we may care to divulge. There *is* intelligence in the vast universe. We may be only its eardrum.

Tell that to some people and you start a discussion that ends up sounding a lot like Mickey Mouse visits the Oracles. But the ears in the valley have a mission. They just listen. Period.

They listen for a response to Mickey Mouse cartoons and Mr. Ed and things like that. In the control rooms nestled in the shadow of the White Mountains, banks of digital recorders and cathode ray tube displays monitor the entire bandwidth. Listening.

In the cool blue of the light, amid the whistle of cooling electronic fans, sits a very fat young man browsing through the fortieth anniversary edition of Playboy. Miss December folds out at arm's length and his eyes cruise between her airbrushed delights.

For longer than he has been alive, slick images of women have caused men to consider their lot in life and eyeball the secretary, their co-worker, with more than aplomb. It is a subtle irony to be working at the leading edge of a technology that may crack open the mystery of the universe and yet, with the majority of one's awareness, be focused on man's most primitive urges.

Attentive enough to miss the first blips that are coming across the ether and gathering in the giant Mickey Mouse ears. A red light in the corner of the room flashes and Miss December drops to the floor as the fat boy spins in his chair.

It was coming in! *Something* danced across the screen momentarily, then stopped. He waited. Almost too good to be true for this to happen on his watch.

Like catching the Japanese on radar before Pearl Harbor.

No mistake here. Here it comes again.

THE ANCIENT PELICAN

I had no clue why, just an impulse, to walk some more, the length of Strand Beach, just a block away. From the top of the south entrance I saw the pelicans, thousands, massed above and on the water close to shore. A natural phenomenon I knew, but one I had never witnessed. I could not get down the 253 steps to the beach fast enough.

It was an air show of extraordinary proportions. Well over 2000 pelicans filling the skies and surface of the water fifty yards off the tide line. The birds wheeled and dove like arrows into the water, feeding of course. Bait fish I assumed. Anchovies one fellow gawker guessed. The half mile long beach was populated with less than a dozen people on this warm late November evening. The mansions which faced this spectacle had not a single face at a single window to witness nature at its most wondrous.

I was reluctant to move on, mesmerized by the spectacle. I walked slowly north on the beach at the edge of the water. It was there, just where I needed to turn to head back up the steps to this long lonely beach that I spotted an old pelican, standing alone on a rock.

I knew in my heart that it meant he was dying. He simply had no energy left to mount the wind and feast with the others. No energy to soar effortlessly the crest of the waves of this or any other California beach. Gone for good was the joy of soaring the cliffs in long formations, his memories of a lifetime of flying, fishing, floating and figuring out where the next meal would come from.

I watched this Ancient Pelican twist his bill around to preen himself as he done all his life. He moved his wings in a pained slow motion as if he could fly once again. He turned his head to watch the sun now low on the horizon as it silhouetted his friends by the thousands in an aerial circus.

I imagined what an Ancient Pelican mind must understand better than I, that the time to die was near, that his last flight had been flown. I began myself to feel old, some kinship with this Ancient One. I wondered how it would end for him. If he would simply sit down on the beach, breathe his last after dark.

Very slowly he raised his straight head up. In ultra-slow motion he moved his head left to right and back to center as if he wanted one last look at life. He looked west, toward the setting sun.

Pausing, without a whisper he took three simple steps toward the water, stretched his wings their full length, and with two slow motion magnificent flaps was airborne in an instant, climbing into the sunset.

I laughed out loud.

The happiest laugh I have experienced in a very long time. Laughed at myself, and with my "Ancient Pelican." Now I followed him closely as he flew south into the gaggle of thousands, circling twice, and finally diving head first like a precision arrow into the ocean.

I smiled every step of the way up the beach stairs to home.

An older man coming down laughed and said, "shift it into low gear." Every thought I had had about this "Ancient

Pelican" was simply my mind ready to accept an illusion I had created.

In an odd yet simple way he had just reminded me age can be an illusion, one perhaps which standing still seems to engender.

And of course, it's okay to stand alone on a beach, whether one is simply a pelican or one who used to think he was an astute observer of all things.

.....Flap ON "old" friend.

LOGBOOK: AGE 16

August 8, 1960: 1AM

Nuns in blue habits. They wash me out with alcohol; it is excruciating. Ask me my name and a flurry of questions. I am sixteen, on my back, looking at the ceiling. There is no need for any of this. I have just come from a dead place, an interstate wreck on a starless night. Does the business of life include paperwork while there is still blood on the gurney? Two dead lying in the median?

There is a young Nun, a ray of light in this dark hour. She talks softly and holds my hand. In her eyes is a love brighter, more enduring, more mysterious than any I have ever known. Her face is framed in a radiant white border. Two nights we spend sitting beside my open third floor window, the Missouri Summer clinking wind chimes in the courtyard below. I have long forgotten our conversations. I loved her.

She had something I could not touch; we travelled very different worlds, yet lived in the same one. I wanted to tell her I loved her. And I did. Said it but qualified it. Subscripted to this time, this place. Here. Now. For what you are doing, for me...my words were inadequate. Bumbling.

Our final evening drew around us close. Her face reflected the light from the courtyard below our darkened room. She took my hand in hers and said nothing. We spoke not a word for an eternity. Only the wind continued its conversation.

IN NO PARTICULAR ORDER

There is no "personal" God. How can God just be personal when we, none of us, are not separated from him? There IS a God who chuckles at our attempts to define, restrict, embellish, or worship in any form. Though I think Cathedrals are pretty cool.

The Universe of all Universes in the inventory is unknowable. And they're all his. Or hers. Or ITs.

Nevertheless, we are One, indivisible from this multiverse.

There is no real ultimate purpose to life. We urgently wish there was. There is purpose in the short term. Survival. With a great sense of purpose of course.

The source of Happiness is knowing that what I do today has consequences.

The source of pain is the recognition that living is short, or seems to be. That some consequences are desired, some painful.

There is only one Life. Each living entity is a branch however remotely attached to that Life. Past lives are molecular memories that feed the sacred tree of Life. Occasionally those memories rise like sap in an individual.

What is perceived as beautiful IS beautiful. Consciousness is taking the lens cover off a camera. We are the cameras. Still, there are many types of lenses and many focal points in the Universe. Measured in billions of light years, or, femto-seconds.

If I focus intentionally on the Beautiful, my life **will** be beautiful.

If I lash my life to LOVE, I will experience the cosmic nod of approval. The smile.

If, however, I don't move out of the fast lane on the freeway, I may get the bird from the guy behind me.

Certain music has the unique quality of harmonizing my life across all Universes.

Time exists merely to train consciousness in the habits of timelessness.

If I can imagine it, it has already been imagined. Therefore all future outcomes are possible, though not necessarily probable. Imagine wisely and write my own script of consequences. Take action. Work for it.

Everything I have said so far is subject to revision. Soon I expect.

By me or someone else. Probably my wife. :-)

NORMAN ZEN

If our logbooks could whisper: small lies /simple joys
occasional truths
a ship of learning
stratals
Norman Zen
a free spirit
bill boards of thought
wonder working
change ancient hatreds
ride the arrow of time Burma Shave signs
Do It Buy it Become it
Woody Allen: Yes, there is a heaven. How far from 42nd
St. and is it open after midnight
durational expectancy: tip the scale of it
aerial odyssey
global scales architects of fantasy
financial landscapes
outside the envelope (we operate) art on an envelope
Department of Whimsy (from the)
madcap wanton abandon witless seasoned simple hearted
mystical fabled illusory chimerical visionary
allegory inscrutable ubiquitous
dime novel horse opera spinner
veneer of reality seamless reality
wyverns anagogical
myth is more powerful than the reality
a marvelous fiction
global ventures account
geographical names
think tank pure conjecture

cash cow
the manuscript fits in the box
hours aloft years on earth
It was one of the best I've ever read
Patterns of: concern; patience; energy expenditure;
directions and destinations
pattern recognition
operate in envelope of opportunity
catchment: wide basin of acceptability
what ifs lateral thinking
provide a thinking package
clear signals
formation flying: a parallel processing engine
no place to hide in this economy
human capital trauma vs episode
critical thinking; ideas; empower workers; information;
lifelong learning
critical mass; critical velocity: emergent pattern of behavior
atomic energy: bonds release inordinate energy
risk free flight: mind only: transition from gravity
freedom: where mind goes, body follows
theory of everything; age of maybe: fuzzy
things that fly: ideas that soar; feelings that pulse
explore repugnant ideas   examine rigorously
Vitamin B Biplane
aeronautical equivalent: time warp; rainbow
visit the "time shop"
co-jointly create
never look back unless that's the way you want to go
penny arcade; Wurlitzer
our destination is yesterday
an inexpressible loveliness   a thing of heartbreaking
beauty
liftoff a moment of unsurpassing glory

guerilla marketing
geese herding the dreamtime
candy bars with memories wrapped around them
test weekend time capsule life
blues flight therapist flights diet ride hangar nights writers
block
gravity day   virtual hangar   spot on hangar floor
St Ex night flight menu
Uplinks (sponsored by)
inspiring alternatives cosmic reset button windows on the
world
Gift of Dreams and flying machines Smiling Biplanes
Biplane Biplane
Oxygen Rich flying stories   Weight of the World
Trim the fat in your wallet   User friendly flying
mental life preservers playful interlude the power pause
shiny reflections   no visible means of support
script writing is play at the edge
speed writing and speed viewing
outtakes in your life rehearsal
Barnstorm Red China Assemble team
mystical chaos mystical recklessness
placebo patches the gene of peace
let's begin with wingovers speed is freedom
leapfrog life with legs of imagination
cosmic panhandler   (in a sky of cloud Gypsies)
ESD-PNX dotted green lines of life in the desert
dusty tragedies in the middle of nowhere
the only green in town is the baseball diamond
Kayak the desert canals   runway arthritis is grass in the
concrete
Lemoore California NAS: I filled a gene pool a kid with
dreams, ego and nasty tongue
entertain me with the truth

a necklace of green speckled emeralds- dry green polished
by the sun and wind
witnessed by the stars   The Astoria Oregon airport
bathroom - a masterpiece
guess at reality   your mission is to discover your mission
it'll bite you on the forearm (vs. the ass) every time
Planet Earth is absolute art.
high flying seed pod transmigrating the planet
short intervals of people connecting
what's new is exciting -the real information superhighway
cross fertilizing cross linking   cross associating creative
linking
there are no sidelines in life   facts are slippery
I wish I had written that (Conceived that) (I could have
written that) I wrote that
I made it up totally.   Blinded by the light a shared universe
is perhaps an oxymoron
spontaneously   benevolent pattern   operative   in   pure
principle
precessional benevolence ephemeralization accelerating
chromosomically honey seeking
pictures on the wall of life
phase transitions at the edge of chaos
complex adaptive systems   delivery of intellectual property
driving forces predetermined elements
micro incubator   imaginations uncorked   possibility
vector space life changing event mystery maneuver
create a life atlas financial landscape
sensitive dependence on initial conditions
fast forward   rewind and rewrite
flight is an original form of gene splicing thought medicine
a Little Rascals Reality is medicinal
a lot of chaff an aerial time share local area astronauts
what separates us from the lentils

emotional abyss half bubble out of plum
searching through titles   history is meaningless in VR
bump up against quantum theory (joy)   tabla rasa cipher
mimic reality now and then   all places are magical
what are the titles of your life's adventures
exercise the ether salmon up the stream of consciousness
biplane soup... journeys across space-time to places our
minds know well
economy of action what would you do to never be bored
why are the answers always in the signs you see billboards
hyphenated life   snatches of conversation
aliens landed, in the dense tulle fog, in Oregon, in the
winter.
creative tension- - creative chaos
live the story, write the story tell the story
ordinary   reality a   peripheral   actor notes   on   a
page clumping system
we're in black and white territory
words are algorithms   simplicity rules (subtle suspicion its
fallacious)
life is best with an infinite series of aha's (large and small)
please enter and tain me
exercise control of destiny = means musculature control,
feet following mind
let the sand castle be destroyed by the tide
enter; ob; re;...tain goals of life
interlocking cycles of change = energy maturing through
time
Gobenas: an inviolate supply of encapsulated articulated
world views
higher level learnings control lover level impulses
life is a pattern integrity
biophilia= desire to be surrounded by other living things

the endless capacity humans have for hypocrisy and self-deception

debt creation = cell block = straitjacket time

central genius inside (a box of cracker jacks)

a mathematically inviolate ration or ratio exists between payday and evolutionary effort

ferry wisdom discovered on yellow pads harmful to environment

fictional becomes the alternative   emotional baggage gets lost on a biplane flight

the new music barely has a name, and when it does, it refers to nature

cerebral symphony   engine of creation   dreams of reason   mindstorms

tag line   the inspiration continues   contained -in-the-mind beliefs

paradise would not be recognizable without people, or planes

someone objected to the church bells on Sunday

what if everyone had to work here   could not retire here not drive after dark

no jet skis, no power boats, write only one letter to the Sounder, no cars

the biplane is like a mayfly   it's a butterfly   the biplanes returning to San Juan Capistrano   timeless miracle

mmmmmm

help to "think" = intellectualize

help to "intuit" = spiritualize

extirpate

once it has been said, suddenly it is available everywhere, morphogenetic fields

no such thing as a conflict; only separate approaches to the same mountain, different views of the same thing

If I make a successful business, it becomes like everything else. Use the B. Fuller approach: what makes sense? to whom and why? spread the idea, whatever way best spreads the idea.

each act of good will has a destiny

not what to think or how to think, but, only that it is possible to think in different ways   an experiment in seeing, an experiment in observation The Supernatural Agency, creating miracle as choice, utilizing intuited knowledge as venetian blinds for the mind

entrapment: infinite patience (the tick waiting years to jump when you walk past)

each moment of your life a brushstroke

Hi, this is Magic Air Tours, the oxygen rich biplane ride that carries you away in "island time" to a place you've always wanted to fly, above the green diamond San Juan Islands. A magical landscape of wind, sky and sea. A page in your life story of inexpressible loveliness from takeoff to touchdown. Come share the Joy. Two can sit by side

You love a lot of things if you live around them. But there isn't any woman and there isn't any horse, not any before nor any after, that is as lovely as a great airplane. And men who love them are faithful to them even though they leave them for others. Man has one virginity to lose in fighters, and if it is a lovely airplane he loses it to, there is where his heart will forever be. Ernest Hemingway

Wonder if he ever piloted a biplane?

OCTOBER 24, 2016

Dana Point 9:22 PM

Solo walk along the bluff beach promenade. Overcast. Zip up hooded sweatshirt on but its mild, barely need it.

Late 1969. Thirty miles straight out over the black Pacific from this very spot, I am alone for awhile, circling at 20,000 feet at max endurance in my A4F Skyhawk, throttle back, engine whispering. I am the duty tanker. The lights of the LA basin fill the front windscreen and I have one non-reg thought on my mind. How much I would really prefer being on the beach, at a restaurant, with a beautiful girl sitting across from me, my order of surf and turf arriving, her Caesar salad laden with shrimp already on the table. We can hear the surf crashing below our open window.

We are going to make love tonight. Get laid. Call it whatever the world wants. Dinner and small talk a small price we are willing to pay in this dance of life, for life, for the stars that fill the darkness above me. Real life.

Tonight, there is a full moon, and Flying Eagle, my A4F relief tanker clicks his mic to tell me he is rendezvousing with me for happy hour. I scan the moonlit sky for him to my port. The carrier leaves a filmy white wake across the ink seventeen miles to the north.

It has been nearly 50 years since that night his engine caught fire behind me; fifty years since I watched him eject silhouetted against the full moon. Fifty years since I circled and followed him down in his chute almost into the Pacific myself. A drama witnessed by no one on this beach 30 miles to the east. Flying Eagle was rescued, we survived the night.

I walk alone tonight, 2016, the memory vivid and visceral. No one to tell it to but myself. The other pilot and I could walk past each other on the bluff tonight, politely nod hello, without a flicker of recognition.

Remarkably, age 72, I still idly wish for that same dinner, small talk, and late-night rendezvous with Love. My heart has beat over one billion seven hundred million times since that dark night. Every cell in my body has been replaced two hundred eighty-two times. So, really, who am I? What has honestly changed?

Everything yet nothing?

...Surf and turf and her smile. Makes me smile still.

Jane dropped an earring in the front seat of Magic...I found it later...

SCARAB RETURN

July 3, 1996

Dear Jane,

Your Scarab is a happy one. He got to fly a couple more times in the TravelAir and spend the night in the hangar listening to "Magic" tell him some marvelous stories from the last 67 years.

Probably happy to get home though, and hang on your ear and listen to you too.

If you listen carefully, I'm sure the other Scarab will be all ears and along about 2AM the chatter may keep you awake.

Thanks again for flying with me and I have to say your smile is infectious................Best to you and Bill.

PURSUIT OF THE MIRACULOUS

Hard to say when I noticed it. Think the first time I was about 16, lying on the side of the interstate looking up at a night sky full of stars. A little fire was burning under the car down the median that had hit us head on. A big diesel truck rolled up and stopped, his headlights illuminating me. Two people were dead in this wreck. I had only a cut under my chin, still tough to shave around today. Lucky kid.

The next time I recall was a moonless night, eighteen thousand feet over Laos, pointed down at 450 knots. A gunner below had me bore sighted. The shells arced up like 4th of July fireworks, singing past my canopy in white profusion. Can't look at the Vietnam War Memorial with a dry eye today. Simply can't.

Driving through Ann Arbor, 3am, April 10, 1972. Couldn't see the road for the tears of joy streaming down my face. We had a son, just born, and Alison was resting peacefully after a long labor.

Miracles.

Raise my antenna. Pay close attention. Watch and I will see them strewn about in chaotic order, marching in quiet cadence on every compass heading. Yet be prepared. They arrive when least expected...

Standing in the hangar, light rain forcing us inside. A tiny five year old girl clenches her mother's hand tightly, and looks at me with deep concern. I casually assure her we can fly in the biplane when the rain lets up. There is a pause, then her voice, soft and innocent.

"Will the clouds hurt my face?"

Pursuit of the miraculous can turn me into butter. Christmas cookies in season. Or save me on the interstate.

Now and then I sit in my hangar, alone, as the sunset casts a glowing light across the TravelAir wings. A solid day of flying under my belt. Passengers whose smiles were expressions of an eternal curiosity spun loose from some unlocked vault. Are not now the moments between miracles, for me, simply brief, unexamined instants?

The rains will come, and with them, the wind. Winter roars its crystal message through hangar walls, and windows frosted beside our breakfast table. The lake today is whitecaps, cloud and Christmas. Frothy iciness delivering Season and wood stove crackling warmth. I hardly know what time or reason is anymore. Locked in an embrace with the miraculous, gloriously entangled within, I will crack a joke to hide behind, steer the conversation elsewhere. No matter. We are several billion on our blue planet. Miracles awaiting every freeing, fleeting thought...

The Magners are well this Christmas. In a miraculous kind of way. We send the Miracle of Christmas to each of you. Shared miracles always make the cookies taste better.

JANUARY 3, 1994

It has been a long time since the last epistle I know, too long. But sometimes you have to wait for the computer to open up. The year 1993 was different for us.

Both my folks passed away; my Mom in March and my Dad in December. The business was good but the weather hampered things somewhat and kept the total passenger count lower. We had raised the rates a little and so we really grossed more for the year than ever before. I earned a little more myself. Also had a nice place to live right on the water with fabulous views from NW to SE. Mount Baker was in all its glory each morning and the Canadian Coastal range as well. Plenty of time to sit and contemplate the universe from a quiet lawn chair. A nice counterpoint to the cockpit which of course, also is a great place to witness the planet. Just noisier. Sunsets were special last year. They're generally incredible anyway, but last year sunsets seemed particularly intense. The rides I gave at sunset just blew us all away.

Reading some of the books last year dealing with the sciences of Complexity and ruminating about life and death and the permanence of little things like Mt. Baker gave me pause. While there is much to accomplish, there also seems much ado about very little. Progress is evolution in its smallest increments. If our purpose is to co-evolve, then the news at night should lead us to believe that the direction we have taken is getting odder by the day. The content of the news is not what we wish to hear I think...

123

WING WREADINGS FOR THE WRIGHTEOUS

Messages from Above the Clouds or TRAVELthAIRapy

E-Mail from around the Globe answered by the Magic One...

Hey Magic, why did you decide to become an airplane? Ernie, Spearville, Kansas.

MAGIC ONE: I preferred visible wings, and the more, the better!

Dear Magic, sometimes I feel trapped in LA. How do I get out of here? Amanda, Wapakoneta, Ohio

MAGIC ONE: Get a magnet, a photograph of where you want to be, write a date on the back of it, and stick them both on your refrigerator. Every time you pour a glass of milk, touch the picture. Drink a toast to your dream. Ice water works too.

Madam Magic, I love to fly, but I can't afford it. Jill, Ahwanee, Tennessee.

MAGIC ONE: Flex and flutter your wings. Look at them in the mirror. You do fly, every day, every night. For the sheer joy of it. So, what is it you can't afford?

Ah Mr. Magic, my bank account never says I have much leftover after paying my bills - what's the deal? Terry, Crockett, Texas

> MAGIC ONE: Money in the bank is like extra altitude when you're flying a sailplane. You only need it if its gonna get you to where you want to land. Once you've landed, you're where you want to be. But there is always plenty-o-altitude anytime you need it. Just look out the window. Join the Sky Bank where living your dreams earns you altitude.

PERFECT PARAGRAPH

Cloud wrestling tableau transitory erstwhile...elixir to remove sorrows - steeped in wonder delirious swept away arching fortress fleeting Henry David Cloud boundary of strange attractor visible/invisible particular/ghost image spiraling double helix disturbance trail of eddy's residue of lift and drag stirred swath of combine harvesting clouds granary for the mind cultivating form liberating molecular tensions measuring chaos taking the measure of cradling breath idling the engine of change polishing the patina of Gods own garden aerial spelunking majestic painting with emotion playing tag among the giants swallowing the rainbow diving through the rainbow rocking chair buddies warm blanket of cloud cooling fog of summer afternoon noble enterprise

That was NOT a paragraph Rod.

OCTOBER 9, 1975

Moraga, California. Patiently awaiting Ryan. Born a Californian, healthy, happy. I have a videotape this time. Number Two. Alison and I have a beautiful second son, have completed our evolutionary roles, replicated ourselves, rounded out our family. He is an angel, conceived at altitude, at Lake Tahoe. Maybe there will be something unique and rarefied for him.

Destiny spinning again across an interstellar landscape to land in his lap or simply flash across his field of vision. I listen to his voice in the delivery room and there are echoes again of eternity. It is that first filling of his lungs with air and his first magnificent Hello cradled in the hands of the nurse and doctor that resonates across all time and through our hearts.

That first moment we know Life has renewed itself again and we are given the chance to Love and be loved and live LOVE.

I am so happy to be a Dad in all this, a minor role no question, yet I relish the opportunity. Yes, he may pee on me when I change his diapers sometime, he may sell lemonade on our front lawn to kids walking home from grade school, he may be a soccer goalie and a catcher in little league, wrinkle the side of our van on his first night driving.

But none of that will matter. We will Love this son into whatever world we have brought him.

The world we ushered Ryan into IS suddenly changing. A few days later, at the supermarket I read the cover of People magazine, recognize a face and scan the article quickly standing in the checkout line. I buy the magazine, only time in my life I buy it.

My path in the world changes once more. An idea bubbles through my consciousness. Around the corner from the market is the Rheem Theater, empty, unused, a movie theater with 1,023 deeply upholstered seats that rock gently back and forth. Once the finest theater west of the Mississippi.

I can rent it for a day for almost nothing, $500. I make a list of the flying films I have always wanted to see on the big screen, a list of people I would like to meet and have speak at my show for that day. Some phone calls, some wild guess work about whether it will work, can I afford this or that, but a week later I have scheduled for January 1976 my very own day at the movies.

I call it the Philosophy of Flight, Film Festival and Free Spirit Lectures. A lesson in overdrive. A leap off a tall building with just a cape. All this with a newborn son at home.

I charge only $15 for a show that will run from 10AM to 10PM. It is something only a pilot can love. I drive the whole coast of California putting up posters in airports, sending press releases to papers and flying clubs and everyone I think might have an iota of interest in my show.

Twelve days before the big day. Only 200 tickets sold. I am going to lose money. I am sick.

The phone rings, someone about how to get a mention in the Datebook section of the San Francisco Chronicle. Deadline is tomorrow, do I have some pictures? I do. I race to the city.

Thursday a week later, the phone rings. Guy asks if there are any tickets left for my show? He has seen the front page of the Datebook which has not yet been published, he works at the Chronicle. I say yes, a few, with a smile.

My phone rings off the hook the weekend before the show.

The day of the show, I have to turn away a hundred or more people. No standing room for a 12-hour picnic inside the theater.

There are still 100 people left sitting in the theater when the last question for my featured speaker is answered at 1AM.

It has been $15 for 15 hours for those hardy souls. The show has been a huge success. My cape has fluttered, and my life has been unalterably changed.

And so has my family's.

We have all charted a new course, one that I hope has a bright future, a compass with cardinal headings glowing in the night, beckoning us to follow.

OCTOBER 29, 1997

FIRST time across the winter boundary of no work, flying just a dimming memory again. Faced with a satchel full of thoughts none of which seems particularly significant to anyone I suspect, except myself.

I am drawing away from the task at hand. The reader suffers. It is not a flaw in the writing, but in the living. Ineptitude in drawing conclusions.

Content to hear others express themselves with words I admire, or dismiss. It is the music that renews me, the bright ideas men of science discuss in odd journals... I would choose to leaven it all with glorious insights, but none reveal themselves to me. It is all circumscribed by the daily advance of the sun across the sky. Nothing more.

One day the leaves are bright yellow and there is darkness early in the afternoon... My shoulder is cold with a dim ache left over from February and lifting crates. Only the clink of firewood and the snapping of fire from the rings of cellulose fill the empty voids. Physical stuff is just physical, not mystical.

Dear Anyone. There is just one thing left. To fly across a sky full of love and abandon. To set hearts on another direction. Not a high-tech thing. Cross the planet in high style. With the moon man on my wing... perhaps.

November 3... Crescent Beach was spectacular today. Low clouds speckled with sunlight, strong south winds. The driveway looks nice raked. Scott and Amy told us about their weekend. Marriage proposal on the Golden Gate at Sunset. Warm and Golden. A crowded Halloween. We worked on the house.

My mood sits atop a rainswept peak.

Winter approacheth.

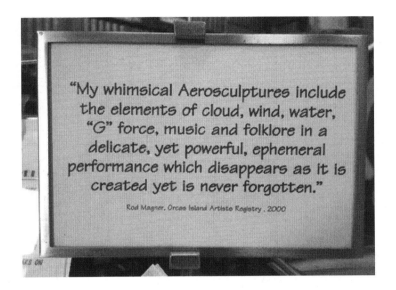

"My whimsical Aerosculptures include the elements of cloud, wind, water, "G" force, music and folklore in a delicate, yet powerful, ephemeral performance which disappears as it is created yet is never forgotten."

Rod Magner. Orcas Island Artists Registry . 2000

MAGIC ONE - THE CATALOGUE

J. Peterman, Wireless, Martha Stewart
Useful items of everyday necessity that help one cope with the rush and tumble of a digital world.

Clothing Items:

The Original Silk Scarf: Embroidered with the emblem of Magic One, done by electronic gnomes in a hidden cave on Mt. Constitution, Orcas Island.

Soft Caps: Smooth to the touch, keep the sun out of your eyes, replete with emblems, logos and one size fits all. All have been dipped in the waters of Crescent Beach and carry that distinctive feel.

T-Shirts: The very original, wildly successful image of Magic One in the brightest red and yellows ever conceived. True to the aircraft, and certain to arrest the eyes of every onlooker.

Sweatshirts: Tiny embroidered essence of Magic tastefully resting on the shoulder, announcing your own Magic. Every shirt has experienced the ferry ride from Anacortes to the emerald islands and been graced with the keen hangar vibrato of engine runups for runway 34 at Orcas' Eastsound Airport.

Essential Magnetic Paraphernalia

Critical refrigerator decor: The truest indicators of ones personal personal ambitions are found on the diary door of the personal food cooler. Dreams magnetically and symbolically held up for all the world to read. "Magic One" magnetic pieces have tested to 99% purity and users have experienced a dramatic 88% success rate. Only the finest lodestone, mined in the magnetic anomaly area at the base of Mt. Pickett is used in the time honored, labor intensive tradition of island miners.

Poster Potpourri

Magic One, The Whimsy: This collection of 10 posters has been regarded in critical circles as the finest in the whimsy/biplane/island category ever created. The genre was set on its tailwheel by the bold, if not subtle, play of wind and wire set amongst the diaphanous words of a yearning public. Hung in highly regarded museums of the world, these limited edition, signed prints seem headed for Christy's Auctions houses, commanding top prices and setting the art world into a wild tailspin.

Magic One, Plant Life: Done to satisfy the demands of customers, this collection of 5 posters was commissioned in the Fall of '92. Each depicts a different genus of the aviators essential biolife and revelry food chain. Unknown for years, these common ingredients found on everyday beaches, taxiways and behind hangar back corners have caused a sensation among mainlanders. For millennium, an island secret, the flying here was so exceptional, the truth became manifest. Lindberg was the first to hint of these things.

Magic One, The Photo: This is the classic black and white shot by the renowned Rahn-on-Buck. In this early picture he has captured what critics have hailed as the best example of "biplane persona." Compared to Mona Lisa in its impact, the camera has caught the perfect moment where Magic One seems to be smiling while her pilot stands idly at the hangar door, unaware of the camera's gaze. Of course, this too is a limited and signed edition, making it hard to keep in stock.

Vintners Propwash: 2 Vintage Editions: Magic One, 1991, 1800rpm and Idle, for the pilot who likes to land slow. The second vintage is a single remaining 1929 Fleet Kinner, bottled in 1976 and awarded aviation's most prestigious and flavorful recognition, The Aviators Anonymous Golden Goblet.

JUST WORDS

it is all spectacle...

I don't live at the edge of the world, but I can see it from here.

where did the music come from, originally? and why?

so Little Magic, what was it like in the beginning?

once you have begun to commute, you are only alive in two places, the beginning and the end of your journey...

"nothing anyone has written or said, matters, except as brick and mortar to your thinking... what you are thinking now is your own..."

of all the children that grew into warriors, how many are children still? Who has outlived the memory of war?

the point of filling daylight hours with pursuits is lost in the very first sweep of tide, the last raindrop to fall from the storm cloud

farfetched... that is, dusted off from light distances, ideas... come smiling to you... I cannot ever repeat the words I love you... if you say them first... I can spin in the light and offer you a reflection of your own radiance everywhere I go. Places. Multitudes. Markets. Hugs. Tears. Anxious eyes. But the giant sun and a Navajo rug are only distantly related.

I do not speak to another in words that shatter reality. It is not comforting. I think that way sometimes though.

across the bandwidth of all space-time is a sinew of light and no light and you can be certain they flicker in your being.

when I am uncertain of a thing, I realize it inhabits an attic of my mind unexamined and perhaps undesired.

Emerson wrote about the affairs of men. We are the part of the grand experiment most easily surveyed. Nothing we propose must be forever. Yet the mountains and the flowers do not bend eternity as we do, and we know it.

what was it I needed to "upgrade" anyway?

I would rather play to an empty theater of one person than to a thunderous gallery of a thousand. Saves on gas, parking, and paper.

THE BABY PRESIDENT

It is these moments I live for now. The hangar quiet, Magic sitting in the May sun, patient. I am in my office, puttering with some detail of no business import, and I hear the door open at the rear of the hangar.

It is a young couple with a tiny baby, three months old, named after a President and sleeping under a floppy hat. Mom is Shelly and Dad is Brian. Travels the world over as photographer. They are from Brooklyn, New York.

Shelly is the picture of motherhood. A beautiful smile, short brown hair, holding her precious child close and uncertain under her loving gaze whether she dare let a stranger babysit while the two of them fly. Brian is much less uncertain, hoping she will let go.

I know in her heart it is asking more than the moment will allow. I love her for holding her ground. I suggest they split the ride and it is gently decided so.

Shelly is eager to fly it seems. She will go first, and her bright smile betrays a fear she will later confess. She does not tell me her fear in order not to restrict whatever it is I will do in the air. She wants to experience it without reservation.

I watch her closely as we takeoff and climb out. Her smile is evident as she tentatively turns her face to the sides. It is cold today and she is wearing open toed sandals, but bundled otherwise in a warm coat and gloves. She laughs at my dumb jokes.

There is a sky full of miraculous cumulus to choose from. I estimate their bases and where I must make my turn to arrive above them, all the while concerned about the cold toes I know she is experiencing. I weigh the time and distance and set the power and climb speed, picking my cloud. My banter is designed to inform, entertain, and help her forget those toes.

We climb to 4,500 feet and as we close on the cumulus giant I have chosen, I tell her what I love to hear myself say, that "it is time for a little Pavarotti, an afternoon serenade." Shelly, this is what flying is all about, a beautiful airplane, a beautiful sky and the world's most beautiful place to fly. I tap the play button on the stereo, timing carefully so that as I finish my words, the music will begin its fade in. The first turn is critical and should be made with the sun and cloud just so, arcing up as the music lifts and reaches a crescendo. It is an arabesque through multiple dimensions.

The cumulus and Magic become partners in a brief dance of love. Shelly smiles and studies wingtips as they brush the cloud. The nose rolls gently as I slide us down the billowing side in rhythm with the music, anticipating a pullup with the next crescendo and matching airspeed to cloud top to soar effortlessly through gossamer crest. I search for narrow holes filled with blue to dive gently towards. Everything depends on airspeed, timing, sun position, cloud edge definition, and the smiles of Shelly. It is a gift from Magic and a sky waiting just for all of us. The colors of love now are filled with music and gentle g forces.

When we land, minutes later, I take her helmet and help her down the wing. Brian and the baby President are waiting. Shelly is beginning to cry, barely able to say to Brian,

"It was the most incredible thing." I am so happy for her. She puts her head on his shoulder and her arms around husband and son, and cries gently, for a long time.

I move off inside the hangar momentarily, letting them be. Embarrassed but thrilled to be part of this gift. I want to hug her and say, "Thank you," for feeling so powerfully about the Magic we've just shared. Yet I don't. Fuss instead, checking the oil with only a glance occasionally from a distance.

Brian is next. We board, start up, and as we taxi away, I glance back at Shelly sitting in the "smart chair" at the back of the hangar. She is nursing her son with a radiant smile. It is a perfect picture. The gift of life passing from one to another. A baby named after a President…it is why I do this.

LITTLE MAGIC NOTES

Air Liberté

Tierra del Fuego...why migrate there....when did the first bird fly, and why? are we not agents of our own destiny?

classroom for liberation: forget gravity, loosen gravity, 100 miles up from here the force of gravity is slight100 feet below the water's surface life is -------

the safest place is right here among the clouds...what chance is there of a lightning bolt in a cloudless sky the trajectory of evolution...are we grains of sand in its path?or sentient beings capable of course corrections

in the cockpit of Little Magic are born the ideas of Air Liberté

we are bounded by the ringed conventions of thought... struck dumb by our limits every day miracles... are these the most remarkable thoughts I could have

is this the most freeing passage of mind I can allow

I grew up thinking I was special... My parents loved me special.... My mother did not intrude on my life, she just launched me it seemed, and had some kind of quiet motherly pride in what I did does the miracle arrive quiet as a cat at your feet?

formation: suspended in space, wingtip to wingtip

carved out of blue nothing, canyons of cloud

ho hum...what is left to figure out, just the minor details of living?

what is the next major breakthrough of mind going to be?

what is the address of the individual who will write about it? certainly someone will speak it aloud, then feel compelled to write it down...or will it be an algorithm so dense only a light speed computer has been able to scribble it down

do not suffer the guilt of cynicism nor the giddiness of light... I love you and I need your love... silence is the end of every conversation

in the middle of the night...ships passing, lives reveling... the high seas, the wide skies, planets spinning... I do not know the why, but feel the "why not" of most of life's inquiries...

trundle off to bed, blast off to the moon, saunter down the walk, takeoff from the runway, ... our words etched in stone sailing forever into the universe...the most intriguing thought... all of our radio transmissions still surfing as energy across the most distant heliospheres...

and yet we can survive here

141

the islands as incubatorial meridians

castaway on Crane Island

a parchment of sky

the participle of our being

TFS: technology fatigue syndrome

who would've thought a model airplane could cross the Atlantic

why would you kill someone when you could instead facilitate their life...

start walking...it is hard isn't it, when being there... and "where" it is, is so important

even if you are connected

i feel embarrassed to even use a cell phone here

the intractable beauty of slowness

masquerading as a biplane pilot, he pressed on

clunk... and the landing

these are the rivets you use to affix to your brain the fuel tanks of your imagination and then you can really arise phoenix-like from the dustbin of history

I had to hold onto that... the old black man in the rocking chair on the front porch of his tin roofed shack in Mississippi... the pace of his life versus mine in the jets....

and now I wonder why it was I had to write about the war experience as I did, just to myself. Here I have ten years of life affirming experiences, and I pen only occasional pages...

Why is it so hard to do what you truly wish to do in life? What roadblocks do we erect, which detours do we accept and plan for?

And the answer it seemed lay 500 years in the future...not my real future you say....no, actually it is MY future...I have chosen it, affirmed it, and it is reaching back to me now and is this very moment opening paths to get me there...The zig zag of the lightning bolt and its numerous branches arc in and connect me...cloud to earth, earth to cloud and cloud to cloud. Drown the bafflements of a world soaked in gasoline and ready to ignite itself. Chose a world where human nature does not play horseshoes with the bodies of the living, hurling them at the stake of prophets.

Choose. Perceptively, Little Magic. The fabric of your life will not be ripped by a nuclear compression of time and light, nor by the ravings of madmen broiling in the sun. There is one great breath to take in life and the oxygen of that moment will sustain whatever choice in freedom you make.

I gazed down the long runway toward the Joy mine for the choosing. Exacting, deliberate, long lasting.

5/2/04: The Little Prince, Asteroid B-612. Texada from 100 miles is Drawing Number One.

You who are so concerned with dying! How did we arrive at this point? By reaching into our future.

"He was no ordinary bird." He was no ordinary little prince. They spoke to us beyond the veils of dark and light. "The thing that is important is the thing that is not seen." The answer is always staring you in the face.

"Draw me a sheep."

Where did the bend begin, the turn that ended life as we knew it, stuffed with anger and frustration and war lords. What evolutionary leap, discontinuity occurred, who put our DNA in a grinder?

Does it matter to you that the sun will go dark in 5 billion years, fry the earth long before that? .... Escape NOW if you must.

Little Magic meets the burka. Makes music among the clouds. The meeting room of the romantics.

Little Magic photographed on the end of the runway 9/11. Draws a sheep. Lights a flame that opens a hole in the fabric of life. All living.

How did we pick up the newspaper and read no headlines or adverse conditions?

It was not about ending war at all. It was about beginning to really live. Fear no war. Through all of space-time. Evil is merely the absence of the blinding light of good

All about me were man made monuments to conflict. Celebrate instead the monuments to living. Sunrises and sundials. Sunsets and surprise parties. Procreation and pan bread.

In the backwaters of living, in a bayou of beauty, cast your fate upon the waters or lift your dreams into the sky...it matters that you place your arms around the incomprehensible.

Do not worry your eyes will dry out. Tears of joy flow from a very deep well.

Pattern/system recognition. The clunk of recognition. The tire chirp of ...."Welcome aboard my magical flying machine." "Welcome back to the planet earth."

So, when did we decide to not do war anyway? Was it a short fat guy with thick glasses that mentioned it? Or was it a pony tailed poet that penned it? Hey, maybe it was a computer that had an electrical short and across the screen came the answers.

Virtual Magic. Pulling contrails of Words spilling out behind her as she carves joy thick in the atmosphere.

Here we are, Above Criticism. Why would we come here to struggle? To tangle?

We are here in the sky to celebrate our mid-course corrections. What you see below you are islands of thought. The dream of people to live quietly as close to the water and sky as extraordinarily possible. And they do.11/17/05

aerial croissants, clouds the puff pastries of an airman's diet

The Bright World. Only necessary to construct your own. People it. Pause it.

Rewind it. Course correct it. Refine and redefine it.

"Let a man in a garret but burn with enough intensity and he will set fire to the world."St Ex. *A Sense of Life.* Pg. 71

I can with a cell phone, connect, anywhere, photograph and send, talk and receive any form of communication.

I KNOW I CAN......I KNOW I CAN

IN THE YEAR 2494

**PASSENGER COMMENTS ON THE PAINTING DONE BY
FRANK LOUDIN**

MAGIC ONE STILL FLIES -- DELIGHTED ALIENS CAVORT IN HER WAKE

MAN LEARNS TO FLY ABOARD PAPER AIRPLANES

ALIENS SURF BEHIND MAGIC ONE

THE WORLD HAS CHANGED

TECHNOLOGY IS STILL BEHIND THE BIPLANE

THE YEAR PAPER FLIGHT WAS BROUGHT TO EARTH

PIXIES CHASE THEIR AERO ICON

EARTH BECOMES A PLAYGROUND

ORCAS FLY-IN HOSTS THE OLD AND THE NEW

FLIGHT REMAINS THE FAVORITE PASTIME OF THE UNIVERSE

BIPLANE CHASING IS CONSIDERED GREAT SPORT

WW 25 IS OVER AND THOSE THAT REMAIN

CELEBRATE

THE YEAR DIET PLANS WORKED ALL TO WELL

SUNSPOT ACTIVITY DRIVES THE POPULATION CRAZY

THE YEAR MAGIC ONE RETURNS FROM

BARNSTORMING MARS

GREETED BY THE FLOCK, MAGIC ONE RETURNS FROM ORBIT

A NEW PHENOMENON EMERGES: PEOPLE WITH

LITTLE TO DO BUT FLY

LOCAL COSMOLOGISTS GREET THE RETURNING

ORBITER, MAGIC ONE

MAGIC ONE ESCAPES THE ORCAS TRIANGLE

PEOPLE CELEBRATE THE DISCOVERY OF PAPERS GRAVITY EFFECTS

THE SPORT OF BIPLANE CHASING REPLACES WAR

HELICOPTERS ARE BANISHED: PEOPLE RESORT TO MAGIC TO FLY

THE LAST BIPLANE DANCES AMONG ADVANCED FRIENDS

CLOUD FRIENDS PLAY TAG WITH THEIR MOTHER SHIP, MAGIC ONE

MAGIC ONE IS LOST AND HAPPY AMONG THE SKY CHILDREN

MYSTERIOUS LAUGHTER FOLLOWS MAGIC ONE ON EVERY FLIGHT

ISLANDERS DISCOVER ADVANCED PAPER AIRPLANES HIDDEN IN MT. CONSTITUTION

MAGIC ONE FEELS THE URGE TO FLY AGAIN

SCHOOLCHILDREN DISCOVER THE TRUE

CAPABILITIES OF NOTEBOOK PAPER

ORIGAMI WAS THOUGHT TO HAVE LIMITS

KINKOS PERSONNEL DISCOVER MAGIC OF

XEROGRAPHIC PAPERS

ATC SCREENS LIGHT UP LIKE CHRISTMAS TREES

VISITORS DISCOVER THE LAST BIPLANE IN THE TIME WARP

SKY PIXIES INDULGE THEIR FAVORITE SPORT

PASSENGERS POINT FROM THE BIPLANE,

"SKY GYPSIES!!"

SKY ACTIVITY AT THE 43RD INTERGALACTIC EAA

FLY-IN

COLLEGE BOUND SKY HARPIES HAVE A LAST

SUMMER FLING

THE SOUND OF MAGIC ONE IS IRRESTIBLE TO THE CLOUD KIDS

IMAGINATIONS UNFETTERED, THE SKIES FILL WITH CHILDREN OF ABANDON

MCDONALDS SELLS THE ULTIMATE TOY

TEAM TRAVELAIR RETURNS FROM EARTH ORBIT

PEOPLE OF THE PAPER MOON BARNSTORM PLANET EARTH

TALL OAK GIFTS FOR LITTLE MAGIC

The tall oak sits on a hill overlooking the airport. Has watched it grow from pasture to pavement. Heard the cough of Cub engines on cold Fall mornings turn to occasional whistle of corporate jets.

"I have a gift for you Little Magic. It is a sea of crunch gold. Leaves which have cleaned your sky and captured the rain, offered you shade on a summer afternoon. They have made a final flight, realized their well understood dream... To twirl and soar in ever so brief a passage from limb to earth. They have only one flight to make in life, and each does it perfectly."

As if on cue, a wintery wind kicks up and fills my cockpit with leafy gold...Today I feel wealthy in ways which matter most...I have many flights to make, one life to *perfect*

I REMEMBER

I remember.

Long ago, in a faraway place, the first smile I made. Lying on my back in the crib, a blue blanket wrapped around me. My Mother's face and my Dad's beside hers. They seemed to be happy, very happy. They spoke in soft words I did not yet understand, but it was the words spoken by their eyes which made me smile.

It was the beginning of many firsts. I remember them all now. Not in sequence of course, but whenever I put pen to paper, nose to air, eye to horizon.

Living is a continuum, unbroken by season or fracture of intent. The heart just moves ahead dancing in rhythm with the stars and all that ever was. As if there were no first or last anything. The beating of my heart opens the windows of perception.

It is there I choose to stand in wonder. As the fog of uncertainty clears, the windows clear glass bears only tiny rivulets of moisture, remnant reminders of that uncertainty.

I remember now.

Mom. Holding me. Nursing. My eyes closed. Utterly at Peace. Just the two of us at home. There is no world order, no written pact for Peace which surpasses that which we felt. The fires of a million suns circled aimlessly around that center of Peace, beholden to its pull. Oh, I know that comfort. Feel it often now whenever I allow it in. Or out.

I call it the Peace of the Note. The sound of a "clarity" whose "note" is never misunderstood.

In the winter I hear it, the snow soundlessly filling the air around me. The winters white note holds the promise Mom made to me. Find the white winter note and hum it softly and it will lead you to Spring.

When I am at 39,000' headed north at close to the speed of sound I recognize that note Mom passed to me. Somewhere it is always winter, some place it is always summer.

It is not altitude that makes it so. Nor is it an alien force. It is the unwavering absolute certainty that joins every sunrise to the next.

I remember one of them now.

HANGAR CHRISTMAS

The hangar was cold. Different than summer when smiling faces and short sleeves filled the hangar. Kids watched the video Those Magnificent Men and Their Flying Machines. Never tired of it. Summer was perfect on Orcas Island. Magic sat in the hangar after sunsets and dripped oil from her breather line into an old tuna can. She had spent the days flying close to the water, over the tops of cumulus, circling ferry boats, popping balloons and tail chasing after a Waco biplane. It was the perfect life. Two souls in the front seat experiencing for the first time in their lives what it meant to breathe the clear air above the trees and ocean. In the rear cockpit her pilot relished his work and polished her so that she shone her very best in the bright and lingering light of the long summer days.

Now it was winter and raw winds rattled the closed hangar doors. The rain beat on the roof and dripped close to her tail where it leaked from above. She could feel her engine contract, the oil congeal. Her wheels had flat spots and transmitted the deep cold concrete secrets. She could hear the other aircraft come and go. The Twin Beech every night picking up the mail. The Caravan blowing jet exhaust under the side door and shaking the south wall. Now and then the Medevac helo hovered across the ramp north of the hangar. Life seemed to move on even in the winter. The Otters whispered as they taxied past for takeoff.

Magic missed the flying. Was willing to brave the grey skies and bristling winds. But most of all, she missed the open hangar door, and the sight of her friends. Winter was a rest, yes, but it was too long. Too solitary.

Her pilot came sometimes to talk to her, pull her prop through, fix little things. They had shared more than fifteen hundred hours in the air and landed together more than three thousand times. She had never used words to tell him how she loved the wingovers they did, or the way she appreciated his mostly gentle landings. But it was Christmas, and they had flown together now for five years. If there was one gift she could give him, it would be to say to him, Thank You for loving me the way you have. She wanted him to know more than anything, that she did hear his words, which he seemed to utter perhaps not absolutely sure she really heard.

Christmas came, windy and cold, shiveringly bleak. Her pilot was in Alabama visiting in-laws, but for her, time and space truly did not matter. The pilot left after the Christmas dinner for a walk alone. In the southern skies, he heard a round engine and looked up to see a biplane headed east. He stopped and watched and smiled. Two teenagers pulled up at the stop sign a few feet away, their radio blaring. The song on the radio was the theme from Those Magnificent Men and Their Flying Machines.

Magic knew he had heard and the hangar seemed a little warmer.

GLENN MILLER: IN THE MOOD: 2:53

To be read with the music playing...

Black and white. Gabardine. Fedoras. Soldiers swaying in erratic circles. B-17's silhouetted against night sky. Smiling guys. Huge grins. Women with hair long in the back, pushed up in front. Black hair. Long skirts. Troops standing in huge crowds at USO show. Cheering. Jitterbugging. Sailors walking into a club. Images of world beyond their control. 1941 Ford convertible. Ship arriving with troops from home. Glenn Miller and big round glasses. Standing on stage and looking back toward audience, big smile wearing Army Air Corp hat. Trombone at the ready in the other hand. The world black and white and grainy. Herky jerky movements. Crowds. Stand up and dance before the pain bloats so big you can't stand it. War. Dancing. Slinky women and Iowa farm boy goes home to high school sweetheart. Reading letters from home. Have we always been at war? Bandanna on heads of women holding rivet guns.

Long pipe of music echoing down corridors of conscience. Cigarettes dangling off the lips of boys with shovels and steel helmets pushed back on heads. Showers in jungle outdoor privy and nose art and wheeling bombs down tarmac; listening to radio huddled in circle Tokyo Rose flash of dogfight wings tearing off flaming Zero and Messerschmitts spinning violently and strafing up the railroad how did they fly through that fireball? Limping home one wheel hanging down, tail half shot off B-17 slow motion landing crews standing beside runways watching sometimes it blows sometimes it doesn't lowering injured off the crippled bomber. Lost in clefts and half notes and fog of cold bloody dreary England and belly of carrier in gray sky; running on ships deck swarming with silver disc props and god you'd better be good and watch out kamikaze flaming toward you pock marked sky of black balls white splash of insanity behind one hits carrier listing now and belching black smoke facts are not valentines for the heart in war. Unreal temporal world fogged by booze and crazies who haven't learned not to follow their leader but the music must change some day and get beyond the jitterbug and there we have it now in the little wars and the buggers still arguing over command and control and resources and liberty and freedom and threats the glory of laying down your life and God its good someone did back in those black and white days. Jitterbug trombones sliding treble in ballrooms making out on the beaches and backseats coming home wounded but smiling proud. Please Lord let me get home and dance, taste my girl's lips again and dissolve back into whatever dim reality was. Slow it down. Please slow it down.

Listen...I hear it all at once. And they're clapping. Quick clips of reunion. Hats thrown in air ticker tape and high heel show lifting off the dock. There is a future now. Holding hands and crying we-just-believe-in-it.

CLARE HELLAR LETTER

March 22, 1996

Dear Clare,

I enjoyed meeting and talking with you today and I will follow up for you on things. I am enclosing a picture from a calendar I produced years ago with Richard Bach in which we used quotes from his book "A Gift of Wings." I think it is apropos to our discussion.

I believe if we imagine the young man or woman who dreams of one day becoming an astronaut as the pilot of that biplane (he often has passengers along who fill that notion too) then the sounds and sights we witness are in a much larger sense, mankind's efforts at perfecting herself - to move us beyond our territorial quibbling and political self-destructions - if we think of the flying in that symbolic way, it will soften the sounds and you may hear as I do a different drummer, resonating with my heart in a glorious symphony.

Our view of the home planet has changed forever now that we have seen it from afar, and these tiny biplanes are in some ways, stepping stones to that bright future. We are free spirits, each of us, circling and supporting each other. Or maybe we're just a bunch of noisy old biplanes lost near paradise... Stop by the hangar Clare whenever you're over this way. I intend to locate a copy of Finney's books. Thanks for the literary invitation.   Sincerely. Rod

FERRY LINE PHILOSOPHY

IT'S dark in the ferry line this pre-Christmas morning. Two red blankets keep my legs warm. My seat is in full recline, neck warmed by a soft pillow wrapped around. Second time since March departing the island by ferry. For the moment, I enjoy listening to familiar sounds of muffled voices, dog leashes and snatches of morning radio seeping from side windows half rolled down. Something about a war brewing somewhere. A winter storm slamming into the northeast.

The bumper sticker next to me is torn but still readable, "The Million Mom March."

Behemoth pickups in line rumble like M-1 tanks, and carry more computing power than Apollo moon missions. Behind me, high in a booth is a ferry cam transmitting a live picture every three minutes of all seven lanes. I can walk back to the booth, smile and wave to our boys in southern California, while calling on a cell phone to warn them I am can be seen on monitors anywhere in the world.

On the seat beside me is a new digital camera accompanied by a manual as dense as the NATOPS manual we needed to fly a Navy jet thirty-one years ago. Stacked with it is a Photoshop manual, an OS 10.2 computer manual, and the "Memoirs of a Superfluous Man" by A.J. Nock.

But I can't keep my eyes open. The digital supercomputing world is cast aside in favor of rest. And contemplation. Ryan is on vacation in Honolulu. Scott headed for New

York on business. The Magnuson cousins had spent a bright fall day with us in October and Joy commented at dinner about having to worry now about her grandchildren going off to a war, which somehow didn't seem fair.

Yes, we've all done enough worrying for several lifetimes; hiding under school desks in the nuclear cold war; planning to drop a nuclear bomb somewhere in China; watching structures crumble, buses blown up.

Makes you ill.

We are not so thrilled by the unchanging news reports. Innate in us is a hidden preference for peaceful daily routines which overwrite and extinguish the brushfires anywhere else. We have unplugged from that grid of angst. It is incredibly satisfying to listen to the wind and dance with clouds streaming through the canopy of our days.

Remarkably, it is neither difficult nor impossible to imagine a Christmas and a world devoid of sword fighting and slingshots. Aircraft carriers rusting at piers, become floating museums. Fighters and bombers bleaching in desert sun.

We have our feet, not our heads, in the rocks and sand of our beaches, our hearts and eyes are trained on the stars, those resident in the heavens, and those living amongst us. It was and is, an easy choice.

I GOT TO THINKING

Had I Been Born in 1902...

If all the people that have ever lived on planet earth formed a mountain called Everest, and those that lived the longest were at its narrow peak, I would grace the very pinnacle in that rarefied space shared with very few others. It may be difficult to comprehend that simple extraordinary fact in this day and age when new technology barely moves our needle of surprise.

I was born when the average life span was close to 60 while we now predict that the first person to live to be 1,000 may already *be* 60. While there are others before me who've lived 115 years, even fewer at the summit of that Everest of Mind and Spirit have experienced the rapid pace of change I've lived through.

The first Rose Bowl was played when I was 6 months old. I share my birth year with the first Teddy Bear, also born in 1902. I have survived 19 presidencies. There were just 45 states in the union the year I first let out a sigh, and Oklahoma, thank goodness, was not admitted until I was 5, in 1907.

The year after I was born, 1903, the dream of man since time immemorial, to fly free from this planet on wings, was given birth as Wilbur *ran* the wingtip for Orville on the first flight of the Wright Flyer. Yet on July 21, 1969 Neil Armstrong stepped off the Eagle lander and walked on the Moon, when I was still a young and vibrant 67. The year after I was born the first movie theater screened the first film, silent of course. I would have to wait 7 long years before the first talkie.

World War I began when I was only 12. And today there are no veterans of that war alive. Digging for the Panama Canal was begun 2 years after I was born. Just as important, Kellogg invented Corn Flakes in 1906 so a four-year-old me could enjoy them. I would have to wait until 1910 though to taste a Life Saver. and wait until I was 16 to bite into a fortune cookie.

The Model T came out in 1908, I rode in one! I had to wait until I was 18 in 1920 to put on a Band Aid.... But the pace of life ever quickens.

When I was 20, in 1922, the USSR was formed; the first American aircraft carrier the USS Langley was commissioned, and the BBC was formed. But in 1928 at the ripe old age of 26 I could now chew Bubble Gum.

In my 30th year, 1932, a scary Brave New World by Aldous Huxley was published while Hitler was given German citizenship through naturalization. But there was still time to listen in the middle of nowhere to the Olympics in Lake Placid or Jack Benny on his first radio show that year or Fred Allen's comedy hour. Ominously though, the first parking meter is put in the ground.

As I turn 50 someone invents Mr. Potato Head while science builds the first Hydrogen Bomb. Which looked like a big potato. But I could have cared less. And though I would not know it then, when I was age 55, a fellow with a first last name, Wilson Greatbatch, would invent the pacemaker. Still, I wouldn't probably need it for about another 50 years! How 'bout that!

Very **very** few individuals in the history of the Universe as we know it, 13.7 billion years old now, have lived as long or through as much dramatic technological change affecting the physical human condition as I have.

The US population when I was born in 1902 was 79 million, today it is pushing past 320 million with the world population sliding towards 7 billion. If my story were a book, now beyond well-worn it would have to tell my story in a simple, profound, and revealing way.

While the Universe spun around me, my Trust never lost its center of balance. I tried to live life as LOVE intended, as my Trust assured me.

Movies, airplanes, cars, computers, potato heads, r/c model airplanes, television and bubble gum, world wars, were nothing compared to the three pillars of my life: Trust in LOVE, family and friends.

AUCTION BARN CAFE

Home Cooking Now Open: Horse Sale 7pm

Highway 114. Roanoke, Texas. Ordered a BLT and Sprite, small. Coffee stains on sugar bottle with screw on aluminum top. Salt and pepper shakers are corrugated glass cylinders. Blue plastic chairs. Trucks roaring past. Can't hear the cars. Brenda, little girl about 5 walks through swinging gate that says "Employees Only" written in black magic marker. Red metal lanterns hang over dining area. They don't work. There are five stools behind a low counter. Kitchen off to right side, big cutout in wall to see through. Only three of us here to eat. Its 11:54am. Sprite came in orange plastic glass with a red and white striped straw. Could smell the bacon cooking.

Man in black felt cowboy hat, dirty, red and white plaid shirt, Levi's faded, scruffy beard about 4 weeks old, cigarette, hair black, curling beneath hat. "What's the special?" he growls. Takes 5 minutes to order, along with his friend Jessie sitting opposite him. They drink from red and yellow coffee mugs. Both order steak sandwiches. Jessie has beard one week old.

Black hat looks at me with a grin and a wink. Lips off to the cook. His sister, it seems. Conversation in dips and snips. Then silence. Both leaning back against the white washed wall. BLT comes without napkins. Red and white checkered plastic table cloths. Tattoo on his left hand. Not two words between Jessie and Black Hat. Chewing on steak sandwiches, legs crossed, boot flicking the air.

Tinny music from radio in kitchen indistinguishable from pans and chatter. "Open" sign flapping in breeze against window. Black hat drives a Chevy Cheyenne 10. BLT just fair.

Auction Barn Cafe. Skip it.

A WINDY PERSPECTIVE

They fill the entire windscreen as you fly north, mountaintops rising islands into the sky. Green fountains of fir and granite slate. Miles of shorelines lapped by cool blue-green Pacific Ocean. Uninhabited at first, the lowlands of Lopez Island lead to a scattering of farms and pockets of human economy. Blakely Island, on the right, thousands of acres until recently owned by one man.

To the west, San Juan Island, whose western shore is where the Orca whales play most often. Stay a thousand feet above them, spot them by the flotilla of boats in pursuit. Keep the tallest mountain to the east if you are headed for Eastsound, Orcas Island.

Expect the winds to funnel down the bay and listen on the CTAF for the islands, 128.25. A dozen airstrips share it. Floatplanes sweep from bay to inlet often below 500 feet. West Isle Air, flying Cessna's on pogo sticks, announce their every intention. To log forty landings on a long summer day is not unusual, bush flying into strips where the public is often not allowed.

Avoid over-flying the 5000-acre Moran State Park on Orcas which surrounds Mt. Constitution. Waldron Island to the west of Orcas is a bastion of quiet. No power, no ferryboats. I get a letter every year thanking me, in advance, for not flying over.

August brings a quilt of morning fog to the southern islands. Lacy tendrils shoot up from Douglas fir as if they are on fire. It is a time to rejoice in the skies above this miracle of geography. My spirit soars on days where cumulus race before a southern wind and below me is a kaleidoscope of emerald and sapphire blue. From the open cockpit of my TravelAir, the scent of wood stove mixes with eagles, occasional bars from Pavarotti in our headsets, and a box-kite of yellow wings aglint in the late summer sun.

To fly in the San Juan's is for me, the gift of all that flight can offer. And a place in the heart where I and my passengers are truly free.

and waiting for the next ride!

CHARACTERS

Potbellied guy from Michigan. Moved here, had $40,000, spent it all on his wife's kidney transplant. Up here to get away for a day. Lives on a small ranch in Enumclaw. Works for Pepsi. Starting a small business in duck quackers. Catalogue business. Thinks this is living my dream. Wants to finish learning to fly.

Couple from Michigan, Ben and Judith. Lansing. Duluth air base. Knew airplanes. Crew cut. Odd teeth on wife. Paints huge landscapes. Talks incessantly. In your face. Nice guy. Well meaning.

Steve Ranker. Just out of USN. CAG LSO, Abraham Lincoln. Ramp strike story of F-14, blue water ops. Wife Beth is flight instructor at Bayview.

Old gentleman from Palmyra, Wisconsin. Knew friend of Richards who loaned him the blue strut for his Parks. Has two Luscombes in hangar there. Lives in Alabama now. Carried picture of a Waco in wallet for fifty years. Tail on shot. Liked colors. Painted his Pietenpol the same blue and white. Stood and talked with Jon and I forever. Wife has horses. Kid lives in Friday Harbor.

Richard and Anne, SF. In wheelchair, MS, she was game. Friend of Ken Cox. Good sport - had some pain, but I think flight did her some good.

Eric Cummings. Quiet, sadness, beard, medical equipment repairman from Skagit County. Celebrating his

170

anniversary. Wife died in accident 4 years ago. Loved to sail in San Juan's. Always does something special. somehow brought up the idea. We talked. Mostly me I'm afraid. Told me his story after the flight. Was remarkably beautiful flight. Over the clouds between Lopez and Blakely with Baker sticking up high above the distant layer. World transformed within a few feet. Lost above the clouds.

LETTER TO LONE PINE, CA

The airplane has unveiled for us the true face of the earth...We set our course for distant destinations. And then, only, from the hight of our rectilinear trajectories, do we discover the essential foundation, the fundament of rock and sand and salt in which here and there from time to time life, like a little moss in the crevices of ruins has risked precarious existence.

Antoine De Saint-Exupery

Dear Lone Pine,

You may never see this letter. It is meant for you, an apology long overdue. I am yet shy and fearful about sending it to you. I flew Navy jets from Lemoore, California. The far side of the Sierras from you. In the summer heat and the winter fog we launched into our playground that stretched from Klamath Lake, Oregon south to the Mexican border.

I flew the A4 Skyhawk, a tiny sliver of a jet with a single seat. We almost always flew in pairs, navigating and chasing each other at 500 feet and 360 knots. It was a challenge. Mind wrenching, incredible fun when I got used to it.

You, dear Lone Pine, whose name forever intrigues me, were a checkpoint, a circle on the chart of towns sleeping on the back side of the Sierra Nevadas: Bridgeport, Bishop, Lee Vining, Mono Lake.

A pilot is a lover. A lover of maps and places and wild terrain. The Sierras rose like a stone curtain from your front yard. Hidden on the spine of the Owens Valley, you promised me adventure. Careening down granite canyons, pulling "G's" in hard steep turns to avoid slamming into them, breaking into the free air of the Owens at your doorstep. That was a brilliant wild thrill, more heart pounding joy than most know in any lifetime.

Yes, I loved the Sierras and they were somehow tolerant of me and my Skyhawk. We rolled across the top of Mt. Whitney; up the flank of the Kern River Canyon with enough speed to roll inverted and arc across the peaks and tuck down into the next winding canyon west.

Even now, years later, as I write this, I am drunk with the memory, the joy of that time in my life. My apology may begin to sound wholly insincere. You must believe me when I tell you this: I love you. I relished the sound of your name. A single dot town population less than tiny. A place to be, once, perhaps for a lifetime.

I met you the first time alone, shining in the early morning winter light. Just at dawn. You lay quiet and slumbering before me, a mile or so distant, framed in the plexiglass of my front windscreen. My Skyhawk seemed equally silent, the turbine at my back barely whispering her song of joy.

On that crystal morning, nothing prepared me for the indescribable portrait of stark beauty flowing by me at breakneck speed. I flew spellbound, in utter awe, breathing slowly, deliberately. Here, now, before me was a town that echoes with its name what all life IS...something alone, solitary, yet parked on a social planet that somehow had to make sense. And at that moment, I had a choice.

I could have said to my companion Skyhawk, "Magic Two, let's not fly over Lone Pine." I should have. I said nothing. Nothing at all. I eased the stick forward, flew down your main street, route 395, low enough to scatter the morning papers. I went to full military throttle. At over 500 mph Lone Pine, you are less than a flicker. At full power, the roar left behind was deafening. Not a soul could have slept through my passing. Not one.

I wanted to shout, to pass reveille, to tell you the world is perfect this morning and you should be up, you should see it. It is magnificent, and you are a part of it. Here is your early morning wake up! Smoke curling from chimneys, dogs chasing down Main Street, the sky is pink and cold and winter fresh. Quick, come with me and see this glorious thing we can share...

It was rude, inconsiderate. Certainly illegal. I looked in my rear-view mirrors, fully expecting to see people shaking their fists at me. An impossible silly thought. In an instant you were gone.

Eight years later we met again, the bachelor jet pilot no longer. I drove north down your Main Street, 25 mph, my Ford station wagon, a wife and two young boys and noise of a different sort. A warm Spring morning in Lone Pine. Restful, beautiful, green, alive, clean, undisturbed. Paradise revisited. The Sierras snowcapped to the West. The Owens Valley stepping into Spring. We stopped for a rest, a root beer. And there, in a corner of the prettiest little park in the world, rested an old friend. A weary Skyhawk, fading gray, standing on spindly legs, quiet as a church mouse. I cried out loud when I saw her.

The boys climbed all over her. I pre-flighted her, kicked the tires for luck as I had a thousand times before. Patted her nose, checked for hydraulic leaks. My head swam with the memories of this valley, of that morning so long ago, of old friends and flights, faces, weather, wind and so many "what ifs." This moment was a gift from Lone Pine which I didn't deserve. Why in my passing here, should I be so touched by time, the grand and simple beauty of your name, Lone Pine, by this piece of soil tucked between two mountain ranges. Is it because we share a love for things unequaled, or wish to be alone in a valley of dreams?

I have come to your fountain Lone Pine, and you have refreshed and renewed my spirit. And here, once locked inside me, comes this trembling apology. Forgive my single trespass so long ago. Where you have "risked precarious existence" you have helped me "unveil the true face of the earth." I am grateful. The beauty we capture in youth is the seed of the spirit we see freed with our learning. And learning just takes time.

When we moved to Orcas in 1989, I met a gentleman who had lived near Lone Pine. He remembered reading this letter which I had sent to the local newspaper there... small world.

TIERRA DEL FUEGO

I feel the link...back to Tiera del Fuego, Argentina and St. Ex. and through the ages clear to this moment which will go forward to all of time... in what subtle ways did the world shift when I flew... or was it just me... part of the mystery is that you really don't know, but you start a cascade of events that ripple through all eternity, or at least through your particular universe... the point of it?... who knows... only to be useful in some intricately frozen way... by personal design... like the songs of all the years reverberating through your consciousness... if I could whisper it just low enough, what would it be... what platitude would it be...not teach, just live by example DEMONSTRATE the principle, that it is what it is...perfect the demonstration...the universes all beginning at the same instant, the singularity...none of us new molecules, just old atoms recycled again and again in an infinite series of combinations, each one a test to see if we can be perfected...

I see this great swirling cold mass of space and emptiness going on forever, purposeless, invisible to awareness... microscopic beyond imagination... there must be a beyond imagination if we can conceive of it...all the inventions are there to spread the gene... across all time... every word is cast in a wind and falls upon the page to say the same thing... listen... it is presumptuous of me to give the lesson... I am so far removed from this... I... most enjoy answers which seem so clear to me... each of us is a sounding board for the other... built around it are stories... we are the storytellers because we cannot find the right words just SO to express at this audible level the depth of the mystery and truth we feel... we try it with love, with religion, with emotion, with jailing, with following our passion, with clever whatever, magic, slight of word...everything is aimed at the heart of existence...total freedom is having no choice in changing truth... to come and to go as we see fit is one orbital ring around the truth of who we are...the answer never comes from outside our walled body...it comes in how that body responds to our thoughts...fluid, rhythmic, breathing... wmwmwmwm... there doesn't have to be a point to all this, only a time to consider it... the world stands out on either side no wider than the heart is wide... there would be formula and tricks of words and we would be drawn in to the story, but it was all a drama that was unnecessary... there was *never* a time when a harsh word was necessary because life though precious, is less so with violence to it...

If the story were to be anything it would have to be honest and reasonable... I could not make it up, obviously... everything I would make up would be dancing around the fire of it... would only be the heat from the fire, not the flame, not the sun unwinding from the dawn of man... if I lived every moment with perfect intention, totally aware, not surfing idly through, but driving quietly, coasting when necessary... doing and demonstrating a self-evident truth of the universe about who and what we were... what would it matter I had no fame, no vast financial wealth, no long trips to other parts of the world...

It occurs to me that if we do reassemble in new forms we are no different than the ants in the giant anthill, each with a mission to fulfill and we may as well just do it... the mission we have is absolutely wonderful... that is, full of wonder... it is simply answering the call of every lepton in our body...it awaits the direction... are we free? ah yes, totally-the new combinations of events and circumstances is a delight to witness in creation... we are part of creation... always have been, always will be... it is not our lot to worry... about the fate of mankind...

It is not our destiny to fret over the loss of habitat...it is our call to look through the mirror of these events to the peace and freedom that resides at the center of our life... here, now, a place it has always been... constant... unerasable... and like a long deep breath, let it out... solutions to problems have never required anything other than this, changing our minds... making a decision...

JANUARY 17, 1994

The elements have always been apparent. The story is always based on your own experience, or the research you have done on the subject... the reason to do this thing, tell this story, is that that is what you must do, in the most efficient cosmic ordering of things. It is communication that reorders evolution... that pops us over the horizon of our limited perspective and launches ideas whose "time" is then said to have come...

Somewhere in the volumes written, there will be a word, a sentence, a paragraph that will move or cross over or create the new supervening order of things...an idea which is completed by your story, your words, your experiences...it is an intricate web of global brainpower and your link is this... think the thought and communicate the love behind it... the lesson you have learned... no one will ever duplicate your life, but they are co-tangent, asymptotic to each other and the effect your story has may belie the force of gravity...awareness knows no recognizable boundaries...

The purpose of the writing is clearly to toss out some ideas and let the world feed upon them for their own purposes... it is critically important that the average person do this... demonstrate his most trusted principle by living it, and through the process of telling his story, expect that another will benefit... indeed, all people be encouraged... though it may be totally unnecessary, since communication will evolve without written forms... in fact, perhaps it is antiquated by ancient standards... but it is hard to deny the efficacy of storytelling when we observe where we are at this point and where we have come from... are we festering sores in our cities, or have they really always been that way?

Wider in scope, modern with wheeled mobility, but nevertheless nearly the same as a Renaissance city... barely different in degree... It is not that there are so many books on the shelves, it is that there are so many that are irrelevant... probably... There are principles that incorporate irrelevance I think... that allow us to thereby make course corrections in evolution... in fact, I am not certain that evolution has a predetermined goal and whether it matters or not that we fail... the universe seems too vast to consider that anthropocentric consideration... it is rather that we have a vast array of choices, and it is the fun of deciding and observing the results that makes life purposeful. It is like a small toy boat on a large pond. Nowhere to go, yet we blow on it to urge it this way or that, because it is enormous joy to see it sail off in our intended direction. It may also be that life recedes from us in layers much like the computer-generated pictures that appear merely a collection of fragmented lines and dots. Only with some effort do we see into the depth of the picture as it forms before our eyes.

There exists a system by which an individual can perceive his role and live happily ever after... It is choice with a large "c". There is a mathematics to it that is quite simple. Like the chaos theory and later the complexity theories. Simple power laws and combinations determine the edges and facets of your life and these chosen boundaries form a mathematical tetrahedron which is the most stable structure in the universe and shows itself amongst the tiniest grains of sand. It works in any life, regardless of perceived circumstance. That is why success or happiness does not seem bounded by physical environment or circumstance, but rather by attitude or spirit.

First you must deal with time. Not ordinary time, but a kind of timeless time. The time where your imagination ends, or fears to imagine. Or says it cannot conceive. You are a part of that time already... you are stardust - were before, and will be again. On a VLS (very large scale) what you do then in time, the time you easily experience, is keep it tied or linked to that unimaginably distant time which with care, becomes your own time scale and teaches you the value of "this" little time you have in visual existence. It is not then some faint far off lighthouse warning you of a shoal, but beckoning you and it is you *now*...

I have always thought you could stretch time or shrink it to suit your real or imagined needs... and I think then it is essential to imagine all of your life as a fragile bubble fresh from the pipe and following the wind for a brief but glorious life which reflects the light of the sun and shimmers in iridescent beauty. Stop time. Run time. Think of time as only the "order" or sequence of players playing a game, which can be changed, is not immutable...

It is not this slippery thing to which you are chained... it is rather this dough with which you can shape your life... it is malleable, flexible... it feels taaaaaactilly wonderful in your hands... you are lost in its beauty- experiencing your OWN piece of clay time... as no one else has ever experienced it. The experience of it is incredibly transforming... because you have stepped out of ordinary cruciform time and are now the master of its feel, its rhythm.

It is something far different than what you have done... Time is more the process of touching and feeling the sunlight and the starlight and seasons and riding the wave or the current and sensing NO SEPARATION. It is the lure of being marooned like an old shipwrecked sailor... There is enough to sustain life almost everywhere on the planet...

And so, you read The Prophet, or the Little Prince, or Jonathan, or a host of other books and what you discover is each came from that timeless reservoir of stories that awaits you when you release the links to ordinary time... Perhaps shed the word, like a snake does its skin... substitute a more appropriate concept...

Time is obsolete. Expand your universe. Do not speak anymore of life or death. Beginnings or endings. Think only of the continuous... evolution, cascading, cycling, rhythms... measure the patterns by the music they create in your head... Dance only on the head of the pin. The pin that points to the heart of universe. Eternally regenerative scenario universe.

It is hard to suffer traffic jams, yet it makes exquisite sense if your mission is to merge seamlessly with all universe beyond your skin... Now we come to system. To trajectory. To aim. To mastery. To human variegation... to fuzzy logic and lines, edges and faces of transparent whole systems. Thoughts stumbling and tumbling across the screen of mind and we are fishing for the big one, the right one for us...any will do, but some seem more correct. Why?

The attraction quotient is simply this: where two will form a vertex - two ideas, two motions, two intuitions...they find a natural affinity... the structure of the universe is just that - all complete in us, in our thoughts, in our ideas, in our imaginings, in our evolution, in our wishing and desiring, in our lusts, our passions... it is the tug of the tide, the notion of the wind, the force of the thunderhead... the sadness of the little one... completion... And we are not heading home... We *are* home...

We are not separate in any form except in a slight degree of imagination... enough that it creates disturbance in the equilibrium of universe, but does not co-opt it... universe allows it... we cannot do anything nature does not allow...

181

so we don't have to worry, certainly... about anything... merely choose the highest and best of yellow roads diverging in a woods...

Telling your stories is not as important as *living* them - in pure principle - whatever that may be... There had to be, must be, diversity, wide and unbreachable diversity among thoughts... the evidence is in us now. There is no danger in repeating ancient wisdom, or creating wisdom one day to be considered ancient... Founding fathers expected there would be greater thinkers than they to come along and carry their ideas further... the writing didn't end with them one hot day in Philadelphia... I'd rather be here than in Philadelphia makes a lot of sense... thank you WC Fields... The question for most is this: how best to communicate your principles, your expression of life... you are a flower in a vast garden, almost indistinguishable from the rest... you are a grain of wheat in a wheat field that stretches across a Nebraska horizon... what distinguishes you?

What separates you? Or should you be content simply to be one with the others... inseparate except to one tongue. One grain of sand between the toes of a beach barefoot lad... a Wheatie in a breakfast bowl... It is important to decide... to hide among the non-separate or to flash out in name and flavor... The planet works, pushes to its surface the rocks buried beneath it. Farmers' fields yield an annual harvest as rich as any product. It comes to this then: CHOICE. Yet, One is not better than the other.

It would be fun then, to see my life follow the story scripted in electrons wouldn't it. Would be fun to read it. Would be great joy to watch it bloom before my very eyes and demonstrate the principle which is for me, universe. To include all, but to see it filtering in playful abandon, the whimsy of evolution, through me... ah, what significance...what relevance... what treasure... what simplicity... utter and complete simplicity... a rose, a

Douglas Fir for intimate friends, a Mt. Baker permanent bookend to my horizon...

I have only room for joy now... only colors and pastels and primaries of 32 million varieties... it is not merely magical, it is timeless... and there you have it... no longer the handmaiden of time, but the partner of eternity bumping against the current of life... and the energy transmuted from stardust through Wheatie to Macintosh to printed page to all evolution makes exquisite sense, an aesthetic beyond blueprint... Re-minders of eternity, of ever unfolding universe.

JANUARY 18, 1994

It is a significant feeling, that of being concerned that what one writes or says is inconsequential. There seems to be a need to frame the message in something to make it more palatable, or soften its edges. Perhaps it is not necessary at all. The story is what carries the message, like water a ship, but the message is clear. An independent system in my analysis. So, we look for interlocking systems which precessionally function. Precession is critical to understanding the written communication. The process is a system and a complete one. It stands alone and contributes by employing forces in creation and distribution. It is not necessary to mince words. Deal straight out. Cut the wasted verbiage. Enable. Prod. Stimulate. Clear the air. Fill the personal dialogue box with purpose. See the activity rattle off the percentages as it is filled. Draw analogy from computer look and feel.

What if your life had the "look and feel" of something more exactly as you picture it should be. The most significant error to address is that which says, I am not sure. How do I know if I like it if I haven't experienced it?

Owning the car is not the dreaming of owning it. The dream and the reality share many things, but the experience of it is not one of those things. The only wish book you'll ever need. The only dream book you'll ever need. Interlocking life stories... from those that pass through the front cockpit. Sometimes I can't remember their names. But I am sensitized to their smiles and whisperings and what is happening. Now and then one will look at me almost constantly. I shut up to try to get them to look outside. We are whistling around the San Juan's and what they see is more important than what I say. Though that may be important too.

There is a sense of wonder about these meetings however. I trust in that meeting, in that exchange which is about to take place. It is so comfortable to taxi back to a quiet hangar and let the sounds of ordinary conversation replace the wind and engine. To listen to the leather and metal. Perhaps I go off with each of them, mentally, and in picture form. Certainly, they will watch other biplanes and remember. They will see aerials of other islands and remember parts. They will remember perhaps one comment, but mostly the flavor of what they heard. As I help them into the front seat: what am I thinking...besides avoiding stepping through the wing and hitting their head...I use the most efficient language developed over the years to make the transition easy...I am fussing in the rear cockpit, hidden from them except my smile. I put on gloves they do not see. I watch the oil pressure rise, then I adjust myself just so. I ask them how they are doing and barely hear the answer... in fact, often I run past that without pausing for their answer. I marvel at the wing color.

Always. I remember through them the anticipation... which I felt with Stu MacPherson on my first biplane ride. A sense of adventure. Sky and planet framed, outlined, highlighted by brilliant yellow wings... (As I walk away from the counter at Sea Tac, I hear him say, he has the best job in the world.)

And I do. I interact with my passengers. Learn from them and show them what is important to me. The cockpit is a bottleneck of time, a twisted now, a brave cocoon-antechamber, vestibule to the unknown— what will the minister speak on today...the cockpit is a bully pulpit, a quiet room on a winters night where the lessons of others comes soft between the pages...black on white, which has not changed much. Is it human nature that is so important, or its trends...many think the basic instincts don't change. The halo surrounding them does however. Our environment, entertainment systems, living systems have moved from square one. There is a large checkerboard of squares now and existence is expanded, at a rate faster than ever imagined. Yet we are prisoner to ancient hatreds, prejudices -arterial blockages, to thinking that will allow us to break clear of destructive energy and magnetically employ only creative and positive-nurturing power. There should be thousands of biplanes giving rides. Sailplanes too. And they should move around the world. Delivering perspective! System. Answering hidden agenda.

So, what does the ride business tell me so far. You fly when the weather is good. You cook at the right temperature. The environment is right for the reaction. For system completion. Nature supplies the awareness ready for change, and I supply with the TravelAir, the mix of gravity and angular rate change demonstrating freedom's several axes in ways they have not experienced. Everyone is recording video or watching flight on television but this is the rendering that has impact. The low level intimates Desert Storm sand blower mission. The cloud dancing shows them sculpturing and freedom to the exponential power.

The wings and the color and the earth in a light show mixed with gravity sideways yet just one g, provides the experience of a kaleidoscope theirs to play with forever. And there is the sound, and the wind, and the vibration. All subtle reinforcing systems juggling the mind and reordering the filters now. It is not a couch safe comfortable-ending drowsy experience... It is an exhilarating makeover of perception - one that registers across systems, completing some, starting others, new facets, edges, new parameters. It becomes light in the corners of life, where dreams had lain dust covered... the prop blast blows away the cobwebs... and light transforms the dream into an image never quite seen just this way... and so it is resurrection light... resuscitation light. It is not me that does any of this... it is the nature of reality that structures it so. Aesthetics brings it to life. Superluminal existence. That begins at the beginning and is continuous through all cycles of mathematical porpoising.

I deal now with a top line rather than a bottom line. The top line is measured in system completions. Where more completion is enabled, nature energetically supports the synthesis. Solar energy is not expensive. Thoughts do not draw down a cosmic account.

There is no rationing of thought, or principles. It is the unique combinations of systems and subsystems which precipitate advance and decline and invoke evolution in our consciousness. Inherent in each system, be it music, flight, ice skating, dancing, painting, or programming, is intrinsic beauty which is a non-quantifiable measure of the purpose of life. Intuition is the auctioneer selling us the future, the past and rattling on in the present.

The price we pay to listen to this universal voice is admission to universe at a fully functioning level. Pure energy, that is, pure intent. It is comforting to think that we have 15 million years before the next cataclysm with the Oort cloud of comets. Man, in that span of landscape, will certainly see some change. And even more fascinating: all of that change is already built into the system...

Egyptians will one day fly... you bet...

What television is telling us, even as they parody future thought and tease the thinking out of us... they are teaching us that visual images are huge in their impact, yet unnecessary more than once... news 40 times a day is 39 times too much... but we are impressed. Instant titles to catastrophic events and CNN with Wagnerian background music. The next great invention will be a personal news viewer that synthesizes all the images from all the news channels (pip picture in picture) and when we feel the urge for them, give them to us ONCE... and when we later turn it on, only new messages or images will come forth, though we can recall stored data.

Human stories will be on separate frequencies. Only events with say, a 6.6 Richter interest scale will beep us or interfere. Our concentration and energy will not be dissipated by advertisements nor by repeated dowsings of hyperbola. I wear now a writer's robe. I think they wore robes when they wrote. Silly thought.

JANUARY 7, 1994

Is it hard to imagine a writer's life? Is the point to entertain, educate, pontificate - is it just regurgitated old ideas, or is it necessary for the evolution of the species - full and rich speculations? What does it matter that I write it down anywhere, or lock it up in electronic limbo somewhere.

The incredible vastness of the stars - the interstellar distances - all aware and converging, collapsing down through every age to this moment, in me, through you, through me to the inter-atomic spaces as vast inside as the stars outside. Where is the edge of my shadow in time - Is time perfectly at peace or at rest in me at this moment, or am I filled with the energy of rage, resentment, disconsolate about the future, victim to the stars bidding, slave to gravity? Does my vision subtend a very brief horizon or does it envelope all space-time?

Does my life have to produce a "body of work"? Or is that the result of waking up day to day and doing Something? Is the passion for my "Work" the only requirement of survival? Does the gazelle readily give himself up to the lion, or does he sprint instinctively away in terror in its excitement? Does the cry of a baby in pain mean anything?

Are we choosing, always choosing or creating alternatives?

Does our contribution have to be something tangible? Would daily prayer for the evolution of mankind be sufficient? Is not prayer sufficient?

Do we tune into other parts of the realm via television, phone, fax, satellite virtual links? What does the warp and woof of space-time hold for us - will I ever understand *curved* space-time? Where did I disappear in my dreams? To what vast terra incognito did I wander? There be dragons? What waits at the top of the stairs? What great good will befall me? What part of me moves deliberately and which is dragged along for the ride? What part of me listens to jazz and which part writes symphonies?

Make the day up of little segments of eating, music, gently reminding yourself that life is good, that loving, actively, the world around you is all that is necessary, that you live as observer to a universe precipitating down to you at this moment which is a miracle, of struggle to energize, perhaps to conserve, to get on with itself and you are absolutely essential to its change... There is no reason to despair, only reason to learn and change, plod forward, at light speed.

Imagination Works!

FORNEY, TEXAS MARCH 6, 1984

Lunch in the "City Café"

Willie Nelson posters, three of 'em. Sign, "Bless this Mess." Forney, home of the Fighting Jackrabbits. We Accept Cash. Farmers National Bank, Forney Branch, calendar. Mounted blue sailfish over sink. Dr. Pepper clock. Three ceiling fans. Orange vinyl seats. Formica tops, ribbed aluminum edges. Half melted pats of butter. Front door sign, "Come in, its Kool." Norris milk dispenser. Sprite, 35 cents. Place full. One man with a suit, fortunately, no tie. Lemon meringue pie sitting out next to chocolate cream pie.

Five women waiting tables and cooking. One is young, frizzy hair, tight jeans. One complaining she couldn't get her a man last night. Laughter. Fifteen booths. Full. Special today, chicken fried steak. Long thin room, most booths against one wall. One guy just hollers his order to the cook. High school girls, three, checking me out.

Sign on door heading out, "Remember the Golden Rule. He who has the Gold Makes the Rules." Sprite in tall blue plastic glass, white straw can't reach bottom. Onion rings size of softballs.

City Cafe, next door to Anderson Clayton Funeral Home, downtown Forney...Eat there!

WINDY RAINY SATURDAY NIGHT

January 25, 2003

When I am in the midst of whatever epoch in my life I am working through I am not generally aware of the turn points and mileage markers coming. Too busy really. Yet there are always those wee quiet hours when I take stock of what has passed before me and measure it. Against the dreams I had, the notions I entertained about what this living is all about. When I was 22, age 36 sounded ancient and impossibly far away. So much to accomplish and a verdant carpet of time stretched over the horizon to get it done.

When I turned 40 I could care less about the big deal it was, which everyone joked about. I didn't think that way, didn't accept convention. Or tried not to. Still don't. Fifty sounded ridiculously old. In 14 months, I will be 60 and I'll be damned but that does seem ancient. Now. Won't when I am.

When I look at the Christmas cards with pictures of my cousins and old friends, I see a lifetime of sunrises under our belts. I see the outer changes. Read, body architectures. What I know for certain is that what was inside my heart at 16 is still there, alive and well today. Chastened some by the avalanche of time, wiser perhaps, yet maybe not. The clock ticks, the heart miraculously beats, the eyes behold the unfolding of my animated dreams, the fears, the loving.

When the mileage markers stream by I look in the rear-view mirror. How much of that highway in the mirror do I remember? How many exits might I have chosen to explore the side roads of existence?

Was I on autopilot too much, hypnotized by the road ahead and the music blaring on my car stereo? What *was* my destination anyway?

Good questions for me on a windy, rainy Saturday January night…

or when polishing Magic!

PASSING UNDER THE GOLDEN GATE

THE HANNA CVA 19

I didn't get to say a proper goodbye to her. I wanted a piece of her Flight deck to put on the wall in my den. And now I miss the view of her island tower, which was all you could see above the railing of the Bay Bridge as you drove across it. Occasionally I would have lunch at Red's Java House on the waterfront, and look across to Alameda where she was berthed, watching her, quietly remembering. I first met the USS Hancock, an Essex class attack carrier, on December 29th, 1969, when I slammed onto her flight deck at over 140 miles per hour. It was the first of more than 150 such beatings we delivered to each other. My first flight from her was on New Year's Day, 1969. A combat sortie with 3,000 pounds of bombs hung under my wings.

The "Hanna" was in the middle of a war, slogging around in the warm blue waters of the Gulf of Tonkin. I was a green pilot fresh from Lemoore. I remember my first feelings for her. She smelled of turbine exhaust, salt spray, greasy food, sweat, and coffee laced with fuel oil. She had passageways that twisted and turned like a maze, that reached up and kicked you in the shins. I never completely learned my way around her and was forever discovering new places, or old unwanted places.

The Hanna was the oldest attack carrier in the fleet. Her keel was laid in January 1943, a year before I was born She was in the battles of the Philippine Sea, Ulithi and Formosa. When I was just a year old, she was hit by a kamikaze that killed 62 men. She was the first carrier to get the "steam" catapult even though she was the oldest carrier around. Only her size gave her away. She was small by modern comparison. She was best as a lover. A lover of the sea. She took the measure of the sea and tamed the waves, rolling gently enough to rock you to sleep. Her hurricane bow was a frightening spot to park a jet on a pitch-black night, but it kept you dry, though one night I opened the canopy only to be drenched with heavy spray. Her boilers were strong and reliable, and only belched black smoke when we were in the landing groove, totally obscuring her flight deck which we were due to hit in seconds. We exchanged words often. Hanna's evaporators were probably the best in the fleet. Boilers need pure fresh water, and so do men, and she never failed to provide it. We never had "water hours" like the other ships, where fresh water was shut off for hours.

Hanna knew what her men loved most. She took them to the tawdry ports of the Far East, Singapore, Hong Kong, Yokouska, and Cubi Pt. She kept the crew cool below decks with the best air conditioning system in the fleet. In our stateroom, we had many arguments about how cold it should be. The lower limit was reached when we had ice in the vents.

The flight deck was covered with teak. Real teak. On top of that, some special concoction for better footing was poured on. Fine when it was sunny, but like a slippery ice cube when it rained. One black stormy night, a young junior officer turned her too sharply, to starboard, she rolled, and one jet slid completely across the deck, slamming into another, driving both of them into the catwalks at the edge. Both pilots ejected, landed in the water, were rescued, while their planes stopped and hung in the catwalks.

The Happy Hanna looked like a lot of other carriers to the naked eye. But she had more going for her. Since 1956, she had called Alameda home. From her flight deck on a clear night, San Francisco was oh so close, a jewel of lights and a siren call for a crewman with liberty on his schedule.

On a large plastic window in "flight deck control" some inspired naval artist had created a grease pencil masterpiece of the Golden Gate: inscribed simply with the words, "Only xxx days left to Home." He penciled in a new number each day. That was our calendar, a slow and arduous countdown. We lived for the time when the count would drop below 200, then 100, and finally, single digits under 10. That count had begun under the Golden Gate westbound.

When I left aboard her for my second cruise in 1969, that count began when we slipped under the bridge. I held a swatch of red on top of my white cap so my friends and relatives up on the center of the span would know which one I was. They waved a huge blanket and let unravel in the wind a couple rolls of toilet paper, some of which caught in our radar antennae. I waved and gulped back my emotions then. The tears would have streaked to my ears in the winds that blew across the bow that day.

Later I stood on the fantail astern and watched the Golden Gate disappear, probably longer than anyone else. I could no longer smell the land and didn't know if I would ever again. So that was what it was like in all the novels, the old stories. I didn't know it then, but it would be 8.5 months before I would be home. Ahead were a hundred flying missions in a war that didn't seem to want to end. I came to know Hanna very well in that time.

From a pilot's point of view, Hanna was many things. From 20,000 feet she was a wood chip bobbing in a blue sea that stopped in the green that was North Vietnam, some 60 miles west. Communist China was closer, Hainan island just off a wingtip to the North. Who was the enemy? I never saw his face really. Did his children play in the waves on the beautiful sandy beaches? Why did the Happy Hanna have to spend 30 or more days at a time churning up the Tonkin's waters?

They were questions never answered. The Hanna simply kept moving, following the bidding of her Captain. She never faltered. She was totally reliable. Only once did she quaver, and that because she had been promised a trip home, only to be ordered back to the shark filled waters of the Tonkin Gulf. She left Cubi Pt. in the Philippines in such a hurry that 200 crewmen were left stranded ashore.

She steamed at breakneck speed all that day, but late that night, she slowed, and finally, after hours of rumor guessing, decoding messages and mutinous talk, the Captain came over the intercom and said, "This is the Captain speaking... Officer of the Deck, right Full Rudder, full speed ahead, were going HOME." The Hanna fairly jumped out of the water. Her crew of 5,000 men were delirious with joy.

Those of us gathered in our stateroom slammed each other on the back, shouted and kicked the bulkheads. No more war, no more bombs, no more flying midnight to noon. Home Hanna, take us home Baby! And she did. Some flew home on the "magic carpet." I rode her for 10 days, tickling the shoreline of Guam where we had a mail call, and Waikiki, where we also didn't stop, but passed close enough to smell the orchids. The grease pencil calendar in flight deck control was single digit; and counting.

The sense of anticipation, the joy of cruising the Pacific at peace and heading home is a feeling only a sailor and a carrier pilot can know. The Hancock had known many men, and I don't suppose my feelings are unique. I loved her but I didn't always want to be with her.

Now more than six years later, I stood on Treasure Island with an old squadron mate, Oink, ready with my camera to film her arrival home for the last time. Just the two of us, standing there in the cool November air, anticipating, remembering how it had been. She hove steadily into view, under the Golden Gate, flanked by a water spouting fireboat.

Suddenly two tour buses ground to a stop behind us, disgorged a million tourists, left their motors running so that the air became diesel grade number one. Are no moments sacred! I laughed at the turn of events, coughed in the exhaust, and we left. Once I had watched Hanna sail west from my T-28 aircraft from overhead at 5000 feet. I had put the plane into a dive as she sailed past Alcatraz, went screaming up her starboard side, aileron rolled the airplane completely as I said goodbye to my friends sailing with her.

From 5,000 feet, as she headed west on the Pacific, I knew intimately the feelings of all aboard her. My horizons had been hers once. San Francisco. The Oakland Hills. They were nicer. But Hanna could not languish in port long. Her delight came with airplanes thundering down her decks, her flight deck crew performing a ballet to stay alive during flight operations.

She was at home on the sea, and she was kind to most that came to know her and trust her. For her to be dismantled seems a shame, an ignominious fate. Life is like that I guess. We all used razor blades then.

It's an old joke that ships get turned into razor blades.

Yet now, when I shave each morning with my two-track blade, I wonder if perhaps some of it isn't from salty Hanna steel.

BIPLAYNUS MEDITATIONS

( )

unseen eyes view each excursion dealing with a small
piece of reality the brain is willing to process anticipation
of moves, inside and outside the cockpit   subtle play
inside-mixture,   trim,   airspeed,   rudder   orneriness,
background chatter on 128.25, we sleep, they swim (the
whales) the perpetuity of events the creation of dreaming,
a mind asleep, working in the theater of light and cloud to
silence aloft, imperceptible to others viscous drag and form
through invisible matter unseen and No-see-ums like a pea
under the sheets, a pebble in your show (shoe) unlocking,
open garden gating, the length of the legs of flight the
climbing slowing and acceleration all terms too familiar,
light on the water reflectivity rolling onto final twitching the
stick just so just so, anticipation of reconnection... you
don't make love at a distance caressing the tires where
does the principle let go...

the   equation   reverses   on   touchdown,
reacquaintance gentle dance down the noise over water
no   words   ground   control   listening   post,   ears   data
gathering unseen aircraft clear of my bubble 5 miles
always the assumption they are same altitude (in a car,
they always are) right of way number one to land assume
we can be seen send out signal the miracle of macro
viewing one week just the view   reconstituted flight
blindfolded take some of the blue of the sky and stir it with
puff pastry clouds there is a color called cu there is an
energy called cumulo... micro to macro flip flop between
layers, micro sky farmer, plow the skies till the aerial fields
plant the seeds of (joy)... is it always parentheses ( ) we
have liftoff... the earth is so flat though I know it is round...
why can't I experience round at low altitude, light in the

dark from water to the land and now to the sky, breathing, flying from below to above, what does it mean to be programmed in our genes (jeans) the stock market a bet on human hope, the arrangement of electrons to resemble an account balance blade of grass, blade of silver pushed by the wind oily rags and the ragwing squeeze them both for joy ( ) nurse log cavernous vault I am up very high and if I throttle back, you cannot hear me, I am watching you (or your earth) and if you see me it is because I am airplane and my arms are 36 feet long and bright yellow(I have always wanted to find out what is was like to fly in your airplane) you mean my biplane: give the flyup comic a chance to state your belief or transform it ( ). Tip the scales, tile the looking glass, alter the continuity a series of posters depicting same tick tock one shirt everywhere in the world is ok.

( )

THE RIBBON CUT

We stood side by side, my friend and I, watching the aerobatic biplane wring itself out high above the TV crews. An hour before, he had begun a performance at the desolate old airport, just for the television people, to create an ad for the next days scheduled airshow. Something tiny fell off his airplane and they called him and said, "Land!" He did. And it was a tail brace.

They interviewed him on TV and he was ok, something he had added that was just a backup anyway and that yes, this kind of flying looked dangerous, but professionals made less trouble of it than it appeared. They rolled the biplane back to the hangar.

He worked on it. Used a lady's wrenches. We forgot about it.

Now my friend and I stood watching him again. An hour later. Would he please do the inverted ribbon cut for the TV crews? They really wanted it for the promo. We knew he was testing it at altitude, making sure it was tough and strong, just to be sure. Before he took off he called his wife. The weather was bad, and he just wanted to reassure her. A kind thing to do.

I asked my friend a simple question. What would happen if half your horizontal stabilizer fell off? What would that do to your control do you think? He laughed and we both shook our heads. We did not know a real answer.

201

The biplane swooped down from altitude and circled wide to line for the inverted ribbon cut pass. He pulled up the nose and started to roll left to go inverted. Something fluttered off the tail. We both said, "Oh OH." Our answer came in a split second.

His nose dropped beyond the point of recovery from the low altitude. The engine surged and revved like an animal screaming. No control. None. The sound of fabric and metal compressing and echoing in death is a loud whumping noise, brief and dusty. Vertically he hit. A moment later, a second explosion, this one black and red and louder. A fireball reached the low overcast.

Then the sound of the firetrucks moving at a snail's pace. The black weather had seemed to promise, now death was caught, in electronic tubes and tape and broadcast to the whole country. Front page sequence photographs too. Other TV stations clamoring for copies of the tape.

The lady walked up to my friend, tears in her eyes. He had used her tools, was her friend, why did he have to die? My friend put his arms around her, this little lady who also flew and with whom he had flown many hours. They were alone now, on the apron, facing the smoking wreckage, his arm wrapped around her tiny shoulders.

I walked away and did not listen, to the conversation between a husband and ex-wife. Surely there was something to say about choosing the time you die, consciously or unconsciously. There was much to say though the words do not come easy with the fire in front of you.

I thought for a moment I saw the pilots spirit float up from the wreckage. I shook my head. Why should it float UP? It seemed though, that he had chosen this time, this convenient drama, to "depart the pattern." It was by choice, by odd choice that he left it in dramatic style.

I seemed comforted some by that thinking, my numbness relieved a trifle. The crying all about me was understandable now. But the feeling in my gut was raw and open and empty. Stomachs do not make sense of fire and deaths. They churn of their own accord.

And my friend and his former bride, Mutt and Jeff together, but for another brief moment in time here, touching again, learning and sharing something deep in their souls. I try to make everything fit into neat categories, to come out logically. Sometimes I can. But this whole day wobbles around like a slowing top, reluctant to be an experience to fill a neat category.

File it under Miscellaneous: Flying. Very Sad. 1977

LITTLE MAGIC SPEAKS

We are friends. Really good friends. He made me out of plywood and conduit and aluminum. Even used PVC pipe ends for my engine. And he painted me like the big biplane he flew. He painted and polished me and gave me a name, Little Magic.

When I was completed in the tiny workshop down by the water, he was very anxious to get me to the hangar and show me off. In his heart, he was a child again whenever he watched the children pedal me around the hangar floor.

I watched him come and go all summer long in Magic One, the elephant ear TravelAir in which he sold scenic rides. I sat in the quiet of the hangar that first summer waiting for him to return so I could listen to the people tell him how beautiful flying in the open air was and how the wind seemed to clear the cobwebs from their vision.

Many evenings we sat together in the old hangar, watching the sunset slimming gold leaf to wrinkly black night. We marked the passage of these moments with good feelings, a sense of timelessness swirling in our midst.

Though there were wars in far off places, here, in the cooling hangar, there was merely silence. A promise that tomorrow would yield more of the same.

Not all promises are kept.

Not all tomorrows are met.

No two clouds are the same. I am Little Magic, and I wished to see for myself, more than anything else, the world beyond my hangar. I am just a pedal plane. Mobile, inanimate, a slave to the muscle energy of children, smiling with delight. When the hangar doors close and my pilot goes home, I am already home. Left behind like a rundown watch.

I decided finally, that whatever laws of physics demanded my role as a quiet little pedal plane, doomed to making circles on the hangar floor and occasionally down main street in the big parade...whatever those laws were, they would have to bend.

The laws of physics are really never broken, merely superseded. I knew this, sure as light bent through raindrops makes rainbows. I wanted to surf on the old principles as far as they could fly me, to an edge of uncertainty. From there I hoped to see the landscape of all possibilities. To look in wonder and touch eternity.

Where do pedal planes get such frivolous dreams? I will tell you it is not from listening to adults on the home shopping channel. Or from teenagers in love. Or even to the lofty buzz of important cell phones.

I heard it from the heart of the first child that discovered me parked in the corner of the hangar. There was no illusion of self- importance in her desire to make me move in concert with her wishes. The emotion closest to perfection in it was joy. Unencumbered by direction, goal, purpose or intent.

The eyes of adults saw "cute" and "darling" which were word-masks for concealing something. The brilliant edge of trust and innocence they long ago lost. But an ember in each of them bursts into flame with the oxygen of that memory, though it is usually lost again in the immediate wind of daily living. Almost in fact with the very next breath. Yet I see it clearly, a tiny window into the soul of the world, where all of the good just IS and the bad simply disappears.

The strangest law of all in physics to me is "growing up."

Actually no one has ever written the law down. Everyone simply follows it. There are numerous little side laws that are written down, about the arrow of time for instance, and the distances between things, even unseen things. "Growing UP," is a given, an inescapable conclusion. Photographs show blurry water when exposed for more than a fraction of a second. A person's photographic history runs from baby pictures to gray hair and wrinkled skin.

So it is in the law of growing up that I wished to pan for gold. And to sail for a distant shore. Paddle my own canoe. To really FLY on my tiny yellow wings of plywood.

I heard laughter in the cosmos the first time I even thought the idea. I call it the cosmic chuckle. There are particles in atomic physics which move whenever its twin moves, separated across vast expanses in space-time. The cosmic chuckle is like that. Think a crazy idea, you hear the laughter.

I chose to hurl myself in the direction of the sigh. To locate the source of the first cosmic chuckle. In the process, I hoped I would not grow up at all.

I call her mother, Magic One. We talk a lot.

I told her my idea and there was no hesitation. She smiled and wished me well.

Airplanes, especially biplanes I believe, have been tuned to hear the music of the universe in ways yet to be revealed.

And so it was I left the comfort of my old hangar home and explored my island and a little beyond.

She did ask me to be home before sunset, as I did not yet have navigation lights.

Mothers are like that.

MARIANNA

Lengthy here because today was remarkable. A word I frequent in my search for adjectives...Monday September 4, 2000.

No rides scheduled. One hangar door open, 10AM, I pedal across the field to Merrill Wien's Stearman parked in the grass. Talk to Merrill about a formation flight for Saturday when my old squadron mate will be here. Copy his BFR date and last medical date to put on my insurance papers in case I have him fly Magic again sometime...I look back at my hangar. My lands! There are passengers there!

Pedal fast as I can back to the hangar. A family of four, two daughters, Chris and Candace the parents, Cammie and Chelsea the daughters. A family of "C's". I tell them the price, expecting a recoil, eyes darting back and forth, and quickly offering them a shorter ride, same price for all four.

He is an engineer, smiles only when math makes sense and solutions rise from a formula buried deep in the brains recesses. Candace, the mother, looks at him. She has been to my web site, at home in Atlanta. She is the decision maker. "Let's do two FULL rides." Good Lord, this is going to cost them $420.

They are quiet while I preflight and talk, twanging the tail wires, show them the oil tank, wipe oil from the leading edges. A little symphony of purpose and praise which Magic and I usually share alone. It is almost as if someone has walked in on us in the shower together. Though we have never done that I assure you.

There are cumulus enough for a hundred afternoons of joy. Some low enough to tickle the tip of Shaw Island. The Father flies first, as if it is written somewhere the brave must demonstrate a willingness to sacrifice themselves for the good of the family. He boards Magic in a slow and calculated manner. Careful, precise, merest hint of excitement in his eyes.

They home school the girls, 12 and 9. I'm guessing they are Baptist, Southern. I will be careful with my jokes. All during the flight, I watch him carefully, hoping I can get him to smile, step out on the wing and let go, or simply relax and let the Magic happen. At the end of the flight, he beams, with an engineer's reserve. And Chelsea, like her father, grins, but adds, "it was really cool."

The second flight with Candace and Cammie is, "remarkable," by contrast. Thumbs up frequently, laughter, huge smiles. The cloud over Lopez is perfection. Mother and daughter exchanging smiles and bursts of exultation. I wrap it up, with their permission, and the kaleidoscope of colors, music and 2g's has them looking at each other with a "can you believe we just did that... WOW."

There is a Beaver parked south of my hangar when we get home. Bob Jones from Friday Harbor. JP Brooks and his son Jordan are in the hangar. JP and I sit and talk about his aircraft diesel engine company, American Airlines (he is a captain) and Concorde crashes. I munch on a sandwich because I have learned that even though I have no one scheduled, something good will occur in the next few hours, and it is best to eat while I can.

Bob Jones walks through the door with a young couple and someone's mother. Bob and I sit awhile, they browse. They are from France. The young French girl, maybe 22, has a "remarkable" figure and is as easy to look at as is Magic... Time passes...

"Bob, do you think they would like a ride in the biplane?"

I have no one on the schedule, it is a magical afternoon, and, of course, she has a remarkable figure. And I am thinking, I would love to show these romantic kids something they have never seen before. It is so funny to listen to their French and watch and read their eyes as they realize that, yes, they are going to fly in this beautiful biplane they have been touching and listening to while I sat and said not a word. So it is done.

I have no idea how much English they will understand. I know they will love the music. There is one cumulus left, over Mt. Woolard. I turn downwind and continue the climb. I listen to the engine and feel the vibrations that change over various ranges of rpm. She is different with her new cam. Solid, but different.

I say a few things to see what English they understand. Only a little. I watch them carefully to sense how they are reacting to turns and sunlight and the wind. I gauge my climb and move west to bring the cloud off my left, so I can roll towards it when the music starts and Pavarotti's first few words will soar across the headphones.

I am embarrassed how little French I know, so I say nothing. This is the dance Magic and I have done so many times, but it is always a different day, a different canvas of cloud. Nothing is the same except the magic.

We, the four of us experience and share this brief four-minute dialogue of freedom and joy. It is for them, it is for me, it will be forever. I will listen to them tell the story in French when we land. It sounds so deep and throaty, so wonderfully French I guess. It was, in a word, for me, "remarkable." And she will look wonderful in the t-shirt they purchase. I thank Bob for offering to pay me but turn him down. There are flights to be paid for, and others to be just given away.

I suspect the pump was primed with the French.

A very old lady and a scraggily haired young man have been photographing Magic as the others are leaving. Now they sit on the couch at the far end of the hangar and talk and reload film. I grab a drink of water and wander over to them. I don't have the sense that they are expecting to fly.

Her name is Marianna and she has a smile and energy that belie her worn out hip. The second sentence from her is that she was a pilot. Past tense. But she loved it. I offer to show her the airplane. In the time it takes to stand up, walk out to the plane and grab a step stool along the way, I have learned a great deal of her flying history. The back country of Idaho, Alaska, aerobatics, Stearmans, famous instructors, all a long ago love of hers that has been buried somewhere, but not very well.

Would she like to see the cockpit? You bet she would.

Energy and smile and a child's enthusiasm. This is fun. She peers into the cockpit a long time, exclaiming and absorbing all the joy of that tiny space. I offer a hand to step down and she tells me she's not ready yet to come down. She has her head back in the rear cockpit.

A moment later she is ready, but there are tears in her eyes. She is embarrassed and says I can't believe I'm crying. More soft tears blended with some kind of pure innocence that began when the universe did.

There is no hesitation from me. The heavens have left my day's schedule as open as prairie for this. "Marianna, I've had people in tears AFTER a ride but not before!" We all laugh, which is the cheeks way of catching tears before they run down too far.

"You need to FLY this afternoon... Will you go around the patch with me?"

Marianna does not have the remarkable figure that the French girl had. She did, I'm certain. She still has a face pretty as a rose, and I love her joie de vie. Now there's a French phrase... why couldn't I have thought of that with the French couple? Marianna looks at me, tilts her head to one side, which is the sort of thing you sometimes have to do when logic and emotion are in a little battle inside your head. She accepts with a huge smile, and I am pleased because for some odd reason, she has *me* nearly in tears.

We fly, and the sky has risen to the occasion and provided a large pillow of cumulo joy above Mt. Constitution. She has told me I can do anything I want with the airplane as I put her helmet on. Anything at all she repeats.

Now there is something happening here which is very extraordinary. I am willing participant. I have been a locksmith all week, unlocking dreams. A customer has shipped me a side of Texas brisket barbecue. Another given me a book. A little girl flown twice with her parents and the parents tell me she cannot stop talking about the flights.

And here is Marianna turning her eager eyes in every direction, taking it all in, remembering, beaming the energy of a hundred suns, a hundred lifetimes. We soar high across the mountain and our waiting cumulus. I do, I really try to do the best I can. Find the nearly perfect angle of sun and cloud and lyric. But there are times when I know the universe has conspired all by itself and I am simply the pudgy slave vehicle of its perfect whim.

Marianna and I wheel and arc across a sun split moment. As we roll away from the mountain top, the cloud has evaporated. The once billowing friend has left no trace. Gone. Have we absorbed all its energy? I know the laws of physics. I feel the love in the equations.

Marianna hugs me when we land. A very long, strong hug. She thanks me for the gift of this flight, and she uses those words. We both understand that it has been even more than that. Unstated, wordless love. Nothing as terrestrial as a male and female connection. Something much more remarkable: Freedom in rare dimensions.

Time passes. Magic waits. Someone has left Duane's hangar open for two days. I lock it. I sit, quiet in my soft hangar chair, thinking.

Soon, I have pushed Magic back into the hangar, called Alison to tell her I am coming home. A gay couple from Minneapolis walks in. One has flown in a Stearman many times. We talk, they leave. Perhaps tomorrow a ride.

I pull the two big hangar doors closed. They return.

How about right now, they ask? I smile. We fly.

COMMAND Z CZ

We make decisions. We take actions. All irreversible. Except on a computer. Command Z and go back one step at a time.

The Universe does not *seem* to have a command z feature. Time *seems* irreversible. We age, maybe we slow the process or its visuals, but we haven't reversed it. Yet.

Answering the question, why is there something rather than nothing? Using my imagination, I can CZ back and beyond the singularity, the Planck moment the big bang began and, CZ, before that.

If there is a God, that God must have been extant before our Universe was even initiated. That is the LOVE with which I am so comfortable. That LOVE is genderless. And infused in every quark that has ever existed, in every Caramone. :-) It is the LOVE from which we are inseparate. There may be another word for it of course.

When we design something to accomplish a task, a steam engine locomotive for example, we go to extraordinary lengths to detail its design. We try to leave nothing to chance so that it will operate efficiently and for a long time. LOVE did that before the big bang. We and every cotton pickin' thing since time began is the efficient result. It was designed in intricate and exquisite detail by LOVE.

One could easily say that LOVE "imagined" the evolution of our minds, our Consciousness. That LOVE gave us what we imagine as free will, choice. And Time. Every single aspect of existence. What we experience is what was designed into the steam engine of Universe in exquisite, minute detail before scenario Universe ever began. Every principle, every law, every change of state, every silly inexplicable conundrum, every fraction of flow and process was accounted for.

For lack of a better concept, it is Perfection.

That is why what appears to be so baffling as wildly diverse religions, opinions, the insurmountable problems of any day or epoch, are, actually, none of those things.

That is why when one *truly* Forgives, the instant understanding is so profound. We have entered in to the essence, the heart, of LOVE as was always intended. We may flail around in our youth, or in our old age, while driving the freeway or working in the milking parlor of our dairy farm. *Any* instant we **can** fully recognize our non-separation from LOVE. It is in that instant we see not with only our eyes but with our pure consciousness and simply KNOW there is no separation between LOVE's consciousness and what we have labeled our own.

The so-called problem of evil. If I want to dance, I need a partner. Or at minimum, some music. Whatever I have chosen, scenario universe provides in one form or another. The music may be lousy. The partner miserably uncoordinated. This dance may now be termed a War. Or a business deal gone sour. A marriage on the rocks. A friendship strained. A traffic accident. An insurmountable problem. All because I simply chose to, dance.

Every aspect of our lives, our existence, was detailed by LOVE to be efficient and long lasting. Peaceful. Frictionless yet *fully* engaged. Infinitely long lasting. It's

215

one reason we don't have to think about our heart beating an average of 100,000 times a day, it simply functions below our concern. Powers us. By our choices we have chosen partners in problem solving. Our concepts of self-enable or effectively disable that problem-solving efficiency. There are some pretty powerful TNT and nuclear concepts which are efficient problem solvers of one kind. Of course, they can create the next problem. The seed is always within.

If I choose to dance, that is, to Live, to problem solve, to fly, I will ultimately have to make many detailed decisions along my path. Course corrections. Each will determine the final result, as does each brush stroke in an oil painting. It is in the heft of the paintbrush, or the sensitivity of my hand on the joy stick, where I will experience the flow of LOVE's pure intention. LOVE is the steam engine of creation working through whatever I am, we are. Am I truly problem solving or working against another, name calling, or, LOVING.

The ultimate CZ in Life is LOVE. It is the final arbiter of every Miracle. Rinse and repeat, Then A Miracle.

AFTERWORD

I flew 1200 hours in the Navy and I flew my TravelAir biplane 7000+ hours. In the Navy I did not really get to know the mechanics and techs that watched over the many aircraft I flew. With my TravelAir I did.

I want to Thank every one of them for the conscientious work they did which helped keep me alive. In particular of course with Magic, these terrific people and mechanics: Peter Downing, Elton Hanneman, Wayne Munich, and Geoff Schussler. All friends. All miracle workers-in-my-book.

APRIL 14, 1970
HOME FROM THE WAR

Best part of any war... coming home!

Made in the USA
Las Vegas, NV
23 October 2021